THE
CHELSEA
MISCELLANY

THE
CHELSEA
MISCELLANY

BY CLIVE BATTY

Vision Sports Publishing
2 Coombe Gardens,
London, SW20 0QU

www.visionsp.co.uk

Published by Vision Sports Publishing. 2007

Text © Clive Batty
Illustrations © Bob Bond Sporting Caricatures

ISBN 10: 1-905326-31-9
ISBN 13: 978-1-905326-31-0

Printed and bound in the UK by
Cromwell Press Ltd, Trowbridge, Wiltshire

Typeset by Palimpsest Book Production Limited,
Grangemouth, Stirlingshire

A CIP catalogue record for this book is
available from the British Library

Mixed Sources
Product group from well-managed
forests and other controlled sources
www.fsc.org Cert no. TT-COC-2082
© 1996 Forest Stewardship Council

FSC

Vision Sports Publishing are
proud that this book is made
from paper certified by the
Forest Stewardship Council

Author's Acknowledgements

I would like to thank fellow Chelsea fans Mark Colby, Dave Key, Des O'Reilly and Bob Wheeler for providing some useful ideas for this book, and for showing at least mild interest down the pub when I bombarded them with Blues trivia. Alex Leith and Nick Worger, despite both being Brighton supporters, also came up with some worthwhile suggestions. Special thanks are due to Chelsea statistician Derek Webster, a Blues fan for over 50 years, who wrote to me pointing out a number of inaccuracies and omissions in the previous edition of this book and suggesting some new entries for this one.

Bob Bond, whose work has appeared in a variety of Chelsea publications over the years, produced some fantastic cartoons for the book, while thanks are also due to my editor at Vision Sports Publishing, Jim Drewett, and his business partner Toby Trotman.

Clive Batty

Foreword
By Ron 'Chopper' Harris

I'm delighted to write the introduction to this book, which is full of facts, records and stories about Chelsea. I'm sure that fans of all ages will find it a great read.

Chelsea has been my club and a huge part of my life for nearly half a century. I was there for 21 years as a player – without being big-headed, I don't think many people can say that – and I loved every minute. During my time there I never asked for a transfer or a pay rise, because the club meant everything to me. That remains true to this day, and that's why I'm always happy to help or promote the club in any way I can – by doing the corporate hospitality on matchdays, for instance, or by attending other events. I've got to say, too, that everyone at Chelsea has always been fantastic towards me. Even now, I have a great relationship with the fans and the reception they gave me when I was presented on the pitch before the 2007 FA Cup Final at Wembley was just wonderful.

I first started going to Chelsea in the late fifties. My older brother, Allan, was already at the club as an apprentice and I was invited to be a ballboy at Stamford Bridge. I remember I was paid three half a crowns (37p) per game, which wasn't bad money for the time.

When I eventually joined the club myself as a 15-year-old I found it to be a very friendly place. The people behind the scenes, like George Anstiss the groundsman and Mille the washing lady, were great to us youngsters and we'd often sit and chat to them over a cup of tea before we went training. It was just one happy club.

What probably helped produce the great team spirit we had was that virtually all the lads in the team that challenged for honours in the sixties and went on to win cups in the early seventies were homegrown. Along with me, players like Peter Bonetti, John Hollins and Bobby Tambling all came through the youth ranks, so we shared a lot of experiences together.

Out of them all I stayed the longest, finally leaving Chelsea in 1980 after making 795 first-team appearances – a club record that, I'm pleased to say, gets a mention in this book. A few Chelsea fans have started mentioning to me that John Terry might eventually overtake me. Well, he's a great captain and I certainly hope he stays at the club for a long time to come – but you've still got a long way to go, JT!

I see I also get a mention as the only Chelsea captain to win a game on the toss of coin of a coin. That was a European tie against AC Milan in the days before penalty shoot-outs were invented and I got the better of their captain, Paolo Maldini's dad, Cesare.

Obviously, I knew about that and about the club's record win – 13–0 against a Luxembourg side in 1971 (even I got a rare goal that night!) – but there are loads of other fascinating bits and pieces in this book which were new to me. I didn't know, for instance, that Bobby Moore, England's World Cup-winning captain, had the middle name 'Chelsea' or that the Blues' first foreign player was a Danish international who played for the club before the First World War. I always thought the first foreigners were Eddie McCreadie and Charlie Cooke – the two Scots who played in the same side as me in the sixties!

Getting back to the present, I've been thrilled to see what Chelsea have achieved over the last few years. It's really been fantastic. A lot of that success has been down to Jose Mourinho, who features prominently in these pages. Some people might class him as being a bit flash or arrogant but I sat down with him over lunch earlier this year and I found him to be a very charming and enthusiastic fellow. He asked me, 'Do you miss playing?' so perhaps he thought John Terry and me would make a good partnership in defence!

Chelsea were very close to winning all four competitions in 2007 and, the way the club is set up now, I can see them going on to even better things. I've every confidence that there will be more trophy-winning tales to add to future editions of this cracking little book in seasons to come.

Ron Harris

— THEY SAID IT . . . —

"Chelsea are being managed by Frank Spencer, the well-intentioned but accident-prone half-wit from *Some Mothers Do 'Ave 'Em*."

The Sun's Steven Howard is unimpressed by Claudio Ranieri, December 2001

"It is no secret that I want to turn Fulham into the Manchester United of the south. When that happens, we will be bigger and more successful than Chelsea."

Mohammed Al Fayed suffers from delusions of grandeur, April 2002

"I don't like all this mixing of food – like the sugar with the tomatoes."

Marcel Desailly turns his nose up at tomato ketchup, October 1998

"Jose Mourinho has denied being over-confident, but he has insisted on Chelsea driving to away games in an open-top bus."

***They Think It's All Over* presenter Lee Mack, November 2005**

"I like to think that, apart from being a bit of a butcher, I've got something else to offer."

Ron 'Chopper' Harris, 1979

"Dennis Wise could start a fight in an empty room."

Alex Ferguson, August 1997

Q: "Who would you most like to spend a Saturday night out drinking with?"

A: "Dennis Wise."

John Motson, Observer magazine, 1996

"In the seventies it was Leeds; in the eighties it was Liverpool; and in the nineties it has been Manchester United. Now Chelsea are the team for the millennium. The team everyone loves to hate, that is."

Ian Ridley, The Observer, August 1998

"Oh no, he's got through. Oh, it's alright, it's only Ray Parlour . . ."

Chelsea fan Tim Lovejoy commentating on the 2002 FA Cup Final on Sky's 'Fanzone', seconds before Parlour scored Arsenal's opening goal

"A man born in Glasgow will die, on average, eight years earlier than a man born in Chelsea."
Good news for local Blues fans, Observer Magazine, September 2002

"My hair is difficult, it's a problem! It doesn't always look healthy. But there's nothing I can do about it. If it was up to me, I would have chosen a different kind of hair."
It's a bad hair day every day for Ricardo Carvalho, January 2005

"Ken Bates is a football cretin."
Martin O'Neill, then manager of Leicester City, after Chelsea had knocked his team out of the FA Cup in January 2000

"You know the expression 'When the chips are down'? In English, the things you use in casinos are chips, but in Italian we call them fish. So I once said, 'When the fish are down . . .' It wasn't embarrassing, but everyone was, like, 'What are you talking about?'"
Former Chelsea boss Gianluca Vialli admits to some linguistic confusion, June 2002

"I don't want to change what works. I just want to help take what we have at Stamford Bridge to the next level. And I want us all to work hard and have a lot of fun doing it."
Roman Abramovich, August 2003

"That new Portuguese bloke at Chelsea. He's got a lot to say!"
Brian Clough, September 2004

"I can leave my bed unmade for a week!"
Carlo Cudicini reveals he is more interested in clean sheets at work than at home, November 2006

"JT does the best talks. He knows how to give it to his colleagues. He's born to be a leader."
Michael Essien on John Terry's captaincy style, October 2006

"At Chelsea, everyone's 'geezer'. 'All right, geezer?' 'Morning geezer'. Some of the foreign boys come in like Sheva, who can hardly speak a word of English, and within a couple of weeks all he can say is 'All right, geezer'."

Frank Lampard, March 2007

"What was incredible was going into the Chelsea dressing room to have a chat and swap shirts. It's bigger than my house."

Norwich midfielder Dickson Etuhu is amazed at how the other half live, February 2007

— UP FOR THE CUP —

Peter Osgood scores in the 1970 FA Cup Final v Leeds

To date, Chelsea have appeared in eight FA Cup Finals, winning four and losing four. The Blues first got to the final of the world's oldest knockout football tournament in 1915, when they faced Sheffield United. The match was dubbed the 'Khaki Cup Final' because of the large numbers of uniformed servicemen in the crowd. Sadly for Chelsea fans, the Blues' defence proved easier to penetrate than the German lines in World War One and the Londoners went down to a 3–0 defeat.

After losing to Tottenham in the 'Cockney Cup final' in 1967, Chelsea returned to Wembley three years later to play arch rivals Leeds. The match finished in a 2–2 draw, the first post-war final to require a replay. The Wembley pitch was deemed too poor to stage the rematch so the replay was moved to Old Trafford. In a bruising, physical encounter, the Blues eventually triumphed 2–1 after extra-time with goals from Peter Osgood and David Webb.

More recently, the Blues beat Middlesbrough 2–0 at Wembley in 1997 to win the cup for a second time. The match is most often remembered for Robbie di Matteo's 43–second goal, the quickest in a Wembley final. Chelsea enjoyed a third FA Cup victory in 2000 in the last final to be played under the Twin Towers. Once again, Di Matteo was the hero, scoring the only goal of the game against Aston Villa.

Then, in 2007, Chelsea won the first FA Cup final to be played at the new Wembley. Didier Drogba's winning goal against Manchester United, four minutes from the end of extra-time, secured the Blues their first ever FA Cup and League Cup double.

The full list of Chelsea's FA Cup Final appearances is:

Year	Result	Venue
1915	Sheffield United 3 Chelsea 0	Old Trafford
1967	Tottenham 2 Chelsea 1	Wembley
1970	Chelsea 2 Leeds 2	Wembley
1970	Chelsea 2 Leeds 1	Old Trafford
1994	Manchester United 4 Chelsea 0	Wembley
1997	Chelsea 2 Middlesbrough 0	Wembley
2000	Chelsea 1 Aston Villa 0	Wembley
2002	Arsenal 2 Chelsea 0	Millennium Stadium
2007	Chelsea 1 Manchester United 0	Wembley

— WHY BLUE IS THE COLOUR —

Chelsea's famous blue shirts stem from the fact that the racing colours of the club's first president, the Earl of Cadogan, were light blue (officially 'Eton blue'). During their inaugural season in the Football League, 1905/06, Chelsea sported pale blue shirts before switching to a darker blue for the first time for the home game against Nottingham Forest on 9 February 1907.

For many years, Chelsea's shorts were white, accompanied either by navy blue or white socks. Royal blue shirts and shorts, set off by white socks, only appeared as a combination together at the start of the 1964/65 season and have since been adopted as the club's 'official' home colours.

— DIDIER'S INTERNATIONAL RECORD —

The African King

Powerful striker Didier Drogba has scored more goals for his country while with Chelsea than any other Blues player. The Ivory Coast player passed Jimmy Greaves' old record of 16 international goals when he found the net in a 1-0 win over Guinea on 7 February 2007. Here's the full list of Chelsea's most prolific international goal scorers:

Player	Country	Goals
Didier Drogba	Ivory Coast	17
Jimmy Greaves	England	16
Tore Andre Flo	Norway	15
Eidur Gudjohnsen	Iceland	15
George Hilsdon	England	14
Tommy Lawton	England	14
Hernan Crespo	Argentina	13
Mikael Forssell	Finland	12
Frank Lampard	England	12

— STAMFORD THE LION – A POTTED BIOGRAPHY —

Matchdays at the Bridge wouldn't be the same without Stamford the Lion, Chelsea's long-serving mascot. Here are a few highlights from the colourful life of the club's favourite feline:

1980 Stamford makes his Chelsea debut, cheering up the crowds watching Second Division football at the Bridge. Within weeks he is featured in the opening sequence of 'Match of the Day'.

1983 A great moment as Stamford appears on the cover of the programme for the New Year's Eve clash with Brighton.

1993 Stamford appears in a special edition of 'It's a Knockout!' on the BBC programme 'Standing Room Only'.

1994 The rise of the Chelsea mascot continues as Stamford gets his own column in the matchday programme.

1996 A makeover for Stamford: he loses his tail and has a mane trim.

1998 Stamford is mysteriously kidnapped during a Chelsea-Arsenal match at the Bridge. After a few weeks he turns up in a package addressed to Sky TV football presenter, and Chelsea fan, Tim Lovejoy.

2000 Stamford beats Carlo Cudicini from the penalty spot in the pre-match warm-up before a home game with Tottenham. His goalscoring exploits earn him a double-page spread in the official *Chelsea* magazine.

2002 In a three-way penalty shoot-out competition at Stamford Bridge against fellow mascots Elvis Junior Eel (Southend United) and Clarence the Dragon (Northampton), Stamford finishes in a disappointing third place.

2005 Stamford's spot-kicking skills let him down again in a London mascot penalty competition won by QPR's Jude the Cat.

2005 Stamford is kidnapped again, shortly before the start of the 2005/06 season. He is returned home a few days later.

— THE BIGGEST TEAM PHOTO . . . EVER! —

The world's biggest ever team photo was taken at Stamford Bridge on 7 August 2006 when 7,000 Blues fans joined manager Jose Mourinho, his squad of players and backroom staff in the traditional pre-season snap. A gigantic version of the original photo can be seen along the outer wall of the stadium, opposite the West Stand.

— A CASE OF DISAPPEARING SCOTS —

For three years between 1975 and 1977 Chelsea entered the Anglo-Scottish Cup, a pre-season tournament involving clubs that had not qualified for European competition. Strangely, in nine matches, the Blues never once faced opposition from Scotland – indeed the furthest north they got was a trip to Brisbane Road for a fixture against Orient in 1976. The other clubs Chelsea faced in the competition were Bristol City, Norwich and Fulham.

The only Scottish side Chelsea have played competitively is Morton. The clubs met in the Fairs Cup in 1968, the Blues winning the first leg 5–0 at the Bridge and the second leg 4–3 at Morton's Cappielow Park ground.

However, Chelsea have played numerous friendlies against Scottish teams. Results include the following:

Year	Result	Venue
1952	Chelsea 3 Hearts 2	Stamford Bridge
1963	St. Mirren 2 Chelsea 5	St Mirren Park
1967	Dundee 4 Chelsea 2	Los Angeles
1974	Aberdeen 2 Chelsea 1	Pittodrie
1977	Celtic 2 Chelsea 2	Parkhead
1980	Raith Rovers 3 Chelsea 2	Stark's Park
1985	Chelsea 3 Rangers 2	Stamford Bridge
1992	Chelsea 3 Dundee United 0	Vancouver
2006	Chelsea 1 Celtic 1	Stamford Bridge

— SONGS SUNG BLUE —

Few clubs' supporters have as many songs and chants as Chelsea's. Here's a top ten of Blues numbers, along with the original songs which supplied the melody:

Song	Original	Artist
La La La La-la-la-la, La-la-la-la, Chel-sea	*Hey Jude*	The Beatles
The Blue Flag	*The Red Flag*	Trad. (Germany)
Carefee, Wherever You May Be	*Lord of the Dance*	Trad. (UK)
You Are My Chelsea, My Only Chelsea	*You Are My Sunshine*	Trad. (USA)
Stand up for the Champions	*Go West*	The Pet Shop Boys

Super Chelsea FC	*The Wild Rover*	Trad. (Ireland)
Gianfranco Zola		
La La-la La La	*I Love You Baby*	Andy Williams
One Team in London	*Guantanamera*	Trad. (Cuba)
Top of the League,		
We're Having a Laugh	*Tom Hark*	Trad. (S.Africa)
We are the Famous,		B. Bumble and the
the Famous Chelsea	*Nut Rocker*	Stingers
Didier Drogba, la la, la	*Brown Girl in*	Boney M
la, la	*the Ring*	

— WHAT A COMEBACK! —

Chelsea have twice come back from the dead to win matches after trailing 3–0 at half-time. On 24 October 1970 the Blues were three down at the break away to Blackpool, but two goals by Keith Weller, a £100,000 signing from Millwall at the start of the season, one from David Webb and an own goal gave Chelsea victory.

Almost exactly eight years later, on 14 October 1978, Chelsea were 3–0 down to Bolton at the Bridge with less than 20 minutes left to play. However, 'Supersub' Clive Walker inspired a dramatic comeback setting up goals for Tommy Langley and Kenny Swain before scoring the equaliser himself. With virtually the last kick of the game Walker drove in another low cross which current Bolton manager Sam Allardyce miscued into his own net for the winner.

On four other occasions, against Sheffield United (1913), Darlington (1988), Cardiff (1984) and Luton (1991), the Blues have fought back from 3–0 down to draw 3–3. In 1985 Chelsea went one better, overturning a 3–0 Sheffield Wednesday half-time lead in a Milk Cup quarter-final replay to lead 4–3 only for Doug Rougvie to gift the Owls an equaliser by needlessly conceding a penalty. The match finished 4–4, but Chelsea won the second replay at the Bridge 2–1.

— GOALS GALORE —

In September 1971 Chelsea began their defence of the European Cup Winners Cup against Luxembourg cup winners Jeunesse Hautcharage. Hailing from a village with a population of just 704, Jeunesse were hardly known in their own country let alone in the wider football world.

Faced by a team of steel workers, a butcher, a blacksmith and a hairdresser, the Blues strolled to a 8–0 victory in the first leg in

Luxembourg. Back at the Bridge two weeks later on 29 September 1971, Chelsea recorded their biggest ever win, 13–0, to set a new aggregate 21–0 record for a European tie. The record still stands today, although it was equalled by Feyenoord the following season in the Uefa Cup. Over the two legs Chelsea's 21 goals were scored by Peter Osgood (8), Tommy Baldwin (4), Peter Houseman (3), John Hollins (2), David Webb (2), Ron Harris and Alan Hudson.

In domestic football Chelsea's most emphatic victory was 9–1 against Worksop in the FA Cup in 1908. The Blues' biggest wins in all competitions are listed below:

Competition	Result	Year
European Cup Winners Cup	Chelsea 13 Jeunesse Hautcharage 0	1971
FA Cup	Chelsea 9 Worksop 1	1908
Football League	Chelsea 9 Glossop 2	1906
League Cup	Doncaster 0 Chelsea 7	1960
Premiership	Barnsley 0 Chelsea 6	1997
Full Members Cup	Chelsea 6 Plymouth 2	1988
Champions League	Galatasaray 0 Chelsea 5	1999
Fairs Cup	Chelsea 5 Morton 0	1968
UEFA Cup	Chelsea 3 Levski Sofia 0	2001
Charity Shield	Chelsea 3 Newcastle 0	1955

— INTERNATIONAL BOSSES —

A number of former Chelsea players have gone on to manage national sides. Most famously, Glenn Hoddle left the Bridge to take on the role of England coach, a position previously held by two other ex-Blues, Ron Greenwood and Terry Venables.

The full list of international managers with a Chelsea connection is as follows:

Manager	Years in charge	Country
Ken Armstrong	Various 1960s/70s	New Zealand
Tommy Docherty	1971–72	Scotland
Ron Greenwood	1977–82	England
Terry Venables	1994–96	England
Glenn Hoddle	1996–99	England
Terry Venables	1996–97	Australia
Mark Hughes	1999–04	Wales
Ron Harris	2001–02	Jersey
Ian Porterfield	2006–	Armenia

— BOWING OUT IN STYLE —

A team of Chelsea players who all made their last appearance for the club in a major cup final:

1. Frode Grodas (FA Cup, 1997)
2. Allan Harris (FA Cup, 1967)
3. Danny Granville (European Cup Winners Cup, 1998)
4. Fred Taylor (FA Cup, 1915)
5. Steve Clarke (European Cup Winners Cup, 1998)
6. Frank Sinclair (Coca-Cola Cup, 1998)
7. George Weah (FA Cup, 2000)
8. Didier Deschamps (FA Cup, 2000)
9. Tony Hateley (FA Cup, 1967)
10. Tony Cascarino (FA Cup, 1994)
11. Scott Minto (FA Cup, 1997)

— CHAMPIONS IN 1955 —

Chelsea: 1955 First Division Champions

In 1955, in the club's 50th anniversary year, Chelsea won the First Division title for the first time. Led by manager Ted Drake and featuring stars such as skipper Roy Bentley, winger Eric 'The Rabbit'

Parsons and future England boss Ron Greenwood, the Blues pipped reigning champions Wolves, Portsmouth, Sunderland and Manchester United for the title in a closely-fought race.

Chelsea secured top spot with a 3–0 win over Sheffield Wednesday on 23 April 1955, and finished the campaign four points ahead of their nearest rivals. After the match, Drake told the supporters: "I have all the honours first-class soccer has to offer – but this tops the lot of 'em. Chelsea are the grandest club I have ever known. I am that pleased that Chelsea have won the title that I don't really know what to say. It has taken us a long time – but then look how long it took Sir Gordon Richards to win the Derby!"

Few Blues fans cared that the club's total of 52 points was the lowest by a championship side in a 42–match league programme. Here's how the table looked at the end of the season:

	P	W	D	L	F	A	Pts
Chelsea	42	20	12	10	81	57	52
Wolves	42	19	10	13	89	70	48
Portsmouth	42	18	12	12	74	62	48
Sunderland	42	15	18	9	64	54	48
Manchester United	42	20	7	15	84	74	47
Aston Villa	42	20	7	15	72	73	47
Manchester City	42	18	10	14	76	69	46
Newcastle United	42	17	9	16	89	77	43
Arsenal	42	17	9	16	69	63	43
Burnley	42	17	9	16	51	48	43
Everton	42	16	10	16	62	68	42
Huddersfield Town	42	14	13	15	63	68	41
Sheffield United	42	17	7	18	70	86	41
Preston North End	42	16	8	18	83	64	40
Charlton Athletic	42	15	10	17	76	75	40
Tottenham Hotspur	42	16	8	18	72	73	40
West Bromwich Albion	42	16	8	18	76	96	40
Bolton Wanderers	42	13	13	16	62	69	39
Blackpool	42	14	10	18	60	64	38
Cardiff City	42	13	11	18	62	76	37
Leicester City	42	12	11	19	74	86	35
Sheffield Wednesday	42	8	10	24	63	100	26

— FANS ON THE BOX —

Celebrity Chelsea fans who frequently appear on the TV in one capacity or other include:

David Baddiel	Bubble (Big Brother 2)	Henry Kelly
Tim Lovejoy	Emma Noble	Bill Oddie
Ted Rogers	Johnny Vaughan	Jeremy Vine

— AWAY AT HOME —

On a number of occasions Chelsea have worn their away kit in a match at Stamford Bridge. These include:

- **Chelsea 3 Moscow Dynamo 3, 1945**
  The Blues switched to their away kit of red shirts and white shorts for this friendly match, allowing the Russians to play in their first choice all blue kit.
- **Chelsea 0 Manchester City 3, 1971**
  Dave Sexton's Blues lost their hold on the FA Cup while playing in their away kit of yellow shirts and blue shorts. Under the competition's rules at the time both teams had to wear their change kits in the event of a clash.
- **Chelsea 1 Manchester City 0, 1971**
  Another visit from City, this time in the European Cup Winners Cup semi-final, and again the Blues were forced to wear their away strip. Under UEFA rules the onus was on the home side to change colours if necessary.
- **Chelsea 2 Bruges 0, 1995**
  Back in Europe after a 23-year break and those same UEFA rules were still in place, requiring the Blues to wear their infamous tangerine and graphite kit for the visit of Belgian club Bruges.
- **Chelsea 3 Vicenza 1, 1998**
  A famous European night at the Bridge saw the Blues mount a dramatic comeback in their change strip of yellow with light blue piping. Since then, UEFA rules have changed to demand that away sides change their colours when there is a kit clash.

— 'GATLING GUN'S' STUNNING DEBUT —

On 1 September 1906 George Hilsdon made a remarkable debut for Chelsea by scoring five goals at the Bridge in the Blues' 9–2 thrashing of Glossop North End. The former West Ham striker, whose quick-fire shooting earned him the nickname 'Gatling Gun', had written himself into the Chelsea books in his very first game.

48 years later, on October 16 1954, amateur player Seamus O'Connell made an equally dramatic entry on to the Chelsea scene, hitting a debut hat-trick for the Blues at home to mighty Manchester United. Sadly for Seamus he still finished on the losing side as United won an incredible game by the unlikely sounding score of 6–5.

A number of players have scored two goals on their Chelsea debuts, including:

Year	Player	Result
1905	Francis O'Hara	Chelsea 6 1st Battalion Grenadiers 1 (FA Cup)
1905	Frank Pearson	Lincoln City 1 Chelsea 4
1919	Jack Cock	Chelsea 4 Bradford Park Avenue 0
1920	Buchanan Sharp	Chelsea 2 Blackburn Rovers 1
1947	Bobby Campbell	Chelsea 4 Aston Villa 2
1964	Peter Osgood	Chelsea 2 Workington 0 (League Cup)
1982	David Speedie	Chelsea 2 Oldham Athletic 0
1983	Kerry Dixon	Chelsea 5 Derby County 0

— THE WIT AND WISDOM OF KEN BATES —

Chelsea chairman from 1982 to 2004, Ken Bates was never afraid to speak his mind. Here are some of his most memorable utterances . . .

"The Romans did not build an empire by organising meetings. They did it by killing anyone who got in their way."
Plaque on the wall in the main reception at Stamford Bridge. It has now been removed.

"It wasn't a football club, it was a social club with a bit of football played on Saturdays, occasionally." **On taking over as chairman.**

"If shutting Chelsea solved the hooligan problem I would do it tomorrow, but it wouldn't." **After a pitch invasion by fans in 1985.**

"Poverty among fans is grossly exaggerated when you see what they spend elsewhere. A small minority are poor and can't afford it."
Dismissing suggestions that Chelsea's ticket prices are too high.

"Our fans were systematically abused all evening without any provocation and yet we were fined. A bit like being in a Nazi concentration camp and being charged an admission fee."
On Chelsea's visit to Marseille in 2000.

"Even Jesus Christ only had one Pontius Pilate – I had a whole team of them."
After being ousted from the board of the Wembley Stadium project.

"Experience shows that after a disaster it is particularly difficult with the Americans, who appear to be quite cowardly despite their Rambo films."
Explaining the fall in American visitors to Chelsea Village after 9/11.

"Makelele? Who does he play for? I've only heard of his brother, Ukelele."
Thoughts on a potential Chelsea transfer target.

"Never spend your money on anything that f****, floats or flies."
Ruling out the purchase of an Abramovich-style yacht after selling Chelsea FC.

"I don't care what's on my tomb. Not that I'm thinking of going. In fact, I'm still negotiating on that with the guy upstairs but we haven't agreed terms yet because Heaven may not be big enough for the both of us."
Fending off the Grim Reaper, 1997.

— GRAHAM'S GAFFES —

With a record four own goals to his name 1970s defender Graham Wilkins is the Blues' very own answer to the hapless *Mr Bean*. The teams to benefit from Wilko's generosity were Bolton (1976), Manchester City (1977), Aston Villa (1979) and West Ham (1980). Graham, though, could lose his unwanted record some time in the future as current Chelsea captain John Terry has already notched three own goals (against Arsenal in the FA Cup and Bolton in the Premiership, both in 2003, and against Barcelona in the Champions League in 2006) and is likely to play for the club for many years to come. Michael Essien, too, will be crossing his fingers that he doesn't add to the own goals he scored against Reading (2006) and Tottenham (2007).

On five occasions, the own goal bug has been catching with a pair of Chelsea players netting at the wrong end:

- On 5 October 1963, both Bobby Tambling and Ron Harris scored for Stoke in a 3–3 draw at Stamford Bridge.
- 11 years later 'Chopper' was on the scoresheet for Stoke again, this time with Mickey Droy, as the Blues crashed 6–2 in the League Cup at the Victoria Ground on 22 October 1974.
- On 27 March 1976 David Hay and, yes, you've guessed it, Graham Wilkins found the target for Bolton in their 2–1 victory over the Blues at Burnden Park.
- On 5 February 1983 Chelsea goalkeeper Steve Francis and midfielder John Bumstead both scored at the wrong end in the Blues' 3–1 home defeat by Derby.
- Erland Johnsen and Craig Burley both experienced that sinking feeling after netting for Coventry in a 2–2 draw at Highfield Road on 4 February 1995.

— OSSIE'S CUP RECORD —

Peter Osgood

Chelsea legend Peter Osgood is the last player (and the only Blues player) to have scored in every round of the FA Cup. In 1970 Ossie scored against Birmingham, Burnley, Crystal Palace, QPR (three goals), Watford and Leeds during the Blues' cup run which, of course, ended with skipper Ron Harris lifting the famous old trophy at Old Trafford.

Strangely, up to 1970 it was not that unusual for a player to score in every round of the FA Cup. The last player to do so before Osgood was Jeff Astle for West Bromwich Albion, just two years earlier in 1968.

— DOUBLE BOOKED! —

On 18 November 1905 the Blues played two first-team games on the same day, at home to Burnley in the league and away to Crystal Palace in the FA Cup.

The double-header resulted from the FA's insistence that Chelsea would not be given exemption from the preliminary rounds of the FA Cup, unlike other Second Division sides, because of the Blues' late election to the league a few months earlier. The first two rounds of the competition didn't clash with league games, and Chelsea were able to field strong teams on both occasions. In the third round, however, the match with Palace fell on the same day as Burnley's trip south. Ordered by the Football League to put out their strongest team against the Lancastrians, Chelsea's FA Cup run came to a premature end as their reserves, including two new players who had been registered at the last possible moment, were thrashed 7–1 by the Eagles. At least there was some consolation back at the Bridge, where Chelsea beat Burnley 1–0.

This somewhat farcical episode caused a rethink at FA headquarters, where a resolution was passed insisting that clubs must field full-strength teams in all matches in the FA Cup.

— BLUE GLOBETROTTERS —

In recent years Chelsea have become one of the most cosmopolitan clubs in Europe, with players arriving at Stamford Bridge from all four corners of the globe. Some of them, at least, have been seasoned travellers from an early age, having left their countries of birth to gain international recognition elsewhere. Here's a whole team of Chelsea stars who were born in one country and were capped by another.

Player	Born	Played for
1. Neil Sullivan	England	Scotland
2. Darren Barnard	Germany	Wales
3. Marcel Desailly	Ghana	France
4. Claude Makelele	DR Congo	France
5. Andy Townsend	England	Republic of Ireland
6. Mario Stanic	Bosnia	Croatia
7. Roberto di Matteo	Switzerland	Italy
8. Roy Wegerle	South Africa	USA
9. Jimmy Floyd Hasselbaink	Surinam	Holland
10. Mikael Forssell	Germany	Finland
11. Jesper Gronkjaer	Greenland	Denmark

— LONG-RUNNING CUP EPIC —

In 1956, years before the introduction of penalty shoot-outs, Chelsea were involved in one of the longest-running FA Cup ties in history. After 1–1 draws with Burnley at Turf Moor and the Bridge, two further matches between the sides at St. Andrews (2–2) and Highbury (0–0) failed to produce a winner. The fourth round saga finally came to an end after 540 minutes, when the Blues defeated the Clarets 2–0 at White Hart Lane. Strangely, Chelsea visited Turf Moor for a league match just a few weeks later and the result wasn't close at all – Burnley won 5–0!

— EURO CHAMPS —

Although the Blues have yet to win Europe's premier club competition, the Champions League, 11 Blues players have won the tournament (or its predecessor, the European Cup) with other clubs. Here's the full list of Chelsea's Euro winners:

Year	Player	Club
1977	Joey Jones	Liverpool
1982	Kenny Swain	Aston Villa
1989	Ruud Gullit	AC Milan
1990	Ruud Gullit	AC Milan
1992	Albert Ferrer	Barcelona
1993	Marcel Desailly	Marseille
1993	Didier Deschamps	Marseille
1994	Marcel Desailly	AC Milan
1994	Christian Panucci	AC Milan
1996	Gianluca Vialli	Juventus
1996	Didier Deschamps	Juventus
1998	Christian Panucci	Real Madrid
2002	Claude Makelele	Real Madrid
2003	Andriy Shevchenko	AC Milan
2004	Ricardo Carvalho	Porto
2004	Paulo Ferreira	Porto

— CLUB V COUNTRY —

Chelsea have played a number of high-profile friendlies against national sides, most notably two games against West Germany in the build up to the 1966 World Cup. On the whole, the Blues have performed well at this rarefied level, as you can see from the following results:

Year	Result	Venue
1958	Chelsea 1 South Africa 0	Stamford Bridge
1961	Israel 0 Chelsea 2	Tel Aviv
1965	West Germany 0 Chelsea 1	Duisberg
1965	Australia 1 Chelsea 1	Melbourne
1965	West Germany 3 Chelsea 2	Essen
1969	Mozambique 3 Chelsea 9	Maputo
1969	Mozambique 1 Chelsea 2	Maputo
1971	El Salvador 0 Chelsea 1	San Salvador
1971	Trinidad 2 Chelsea 3	Port of Spain
1978	Malawi 1 Chelsea 6	Kingston
1979	Chelsea 3 China 1	Stamford Bridge
1983	Chelsea 1 Bahrain 0	Harlow
1986	Iraq 1 Chelsea 1	Baghdad
1997	Brunei 0 Chelsea 6	Brunei
1997	Thailand 0 Chelsea 1	Bangkok

— GOAL-FILLED 45 MINUTES —

The most goals the Blues have scored in a single half is seven, in the second half of their record-breaking 13-0 victory over Luxembourg side Jeunesse Hautcharage in the European Cup Winners Cup first round second leg on 29 September 1971. On four other occasions Chelsea have scored six goals in a half:

Year	Half	Score	Final result
1906	1st	Chelsea 6 Glossop North End 2	9-2
1961	2nd	Newcastle 1 Chelsea 6	1-6
1971	1st	J. Hautcharage 0 Chelsea 6	0-8
1971	1st	Chelsea 6 J. Hautcharage 0	13-0

More recently, Chelsea have twice scored five goals in a half of Premiership football. On 6 December 1997 the Blues were drawing 1-1 away to Tottenham at half-time but went on to win the match 6-1, lanky Norwegian striker Tore Andre Flo hitting a hat-trick. Then, on 15 October 2005, the Blues were a goal down at home to Bolton at half-time. Thanks partly to a tactical switch by manager Jose Mourinho, Chelsea recovered to win the match 5-1.

— RED GIFTS —

Chelsea fans aren't complaining, but for some weird reason Manchester United players have had an odd habit of donating own goals to the Blues. To date, five United players have kindly hit the back of the net for Chelsea – and Henning Berg, bless him, has somehow managed the same trick twice:

Year	Own Goal by	Result
1966	Pat Crerand	Man United 1 Chelsea 1
1987	Gary Walsh	Man United 3 Chelsea 1
1990	Gary Pallister	Man United 2 Chelsea 3
1992	Mal Donaghy	Man United 1 Chelsea 1
1997	Henning Berg	Man United 2 Chelsea 2
1999	Henning Berg	Chelsea 5 Man United 0

— ONE MINUTE OF FAME —

On 22 April 1997, 18-year-old striker Joe Sheerin made his Chelsea debut as a substitute for Gianfranco Zola in the 90th minute of the Blues' 1–0 win against Wimbledon at Selhurst Park. It was a big moment for the rookie forward, but he didn't get a touch of the ball before the final whistle blew and never appeared in the first team again. Still, at least Sheerin, who in a quirk of fate went on to play for AFC Wimbledon, could console himself with the thought that he holds the record for the shortest ever Chelsea playing career.

The ten Blues players to have played just one game for the club as substitute are . . .

Player	Year	Against	Player Replaced
Roger Wosahlo	1967	Stoke City (H)	Jim Thomson
Jimmy Clare	1980	Bolton Wanderers (A)	Clive Walker
Gerry Peyton	1992	Sheffield Wednesday (H)	Dmitri Kharine
Steve Livingstone	1993	Manchester United (A)	Neil Shipperley
Joe Sheerin	1997	Wimbledon (A)	Gianfranco Zola
Steve Hampshire	1997	Blackburn (H) Lge Cup	Mark Hughes
Leon Knight	2001	Levski Sofia (A) UEFA Cup	Gianfranco Zola
Anthony Grant	2005	Manchester United (A)	Joe Cole
Jimmy Smith	2006	Newcastle United (A)	Ricardo Carvalho
Sam Hutchinson	2007	Everton (H)	Wayne Bridge

— CHELSEA IN THE WHITE HOUSE —

In 1992, when Bill Clinton became American President, Blues fans were intrigued to learn that the Clintons had a daughter called Chelsea. Some supporters immediately assumed that this was a clear sign that the new incumbent at the White House was a fellow Blue. After all, hadn't Bill lived in Oxford, only an hour's drive from the Bridge, during his student days (when, famously, he had smoked pot but hadn't 'inhaled')?

However, Clinton soon revealed the real reason why he and his wife, Hilary, had named their daughter 'Chelsea' – and it had nothing to do with the football club. Instead, Bill and Hil had chosen the name after their favourite song, *Chelsea Morning* by Canadian singer Joni Mitchell (although, wisely, they decided to drop the 'Morning' bit). Nevertheless, Ms Clinton joins a short list of famous people who are lucky enough to be able to say, 'Chelsea is my name':

Name	Profession
Bobby Frederick Chelsea Moore	England football captain
Viscount Chelsea	Aristocrat
Chelsea Field	Actress
Chelsea Beauchamp	Singer
Chelsea Noble	Actress
Chelsy Davy (c'mon, girl, get the spelling right!)	Girlfriend of Prince Harry
Chelsea Cooley	Miss USA 2005

— PREMIERSHIP POINTS —

Chelsea have been ever-presents in the Premiership since it was formed in 1992 and, statistically speaking, are currently the third most successful side in the history of the competition. As the table (below) illustrates, the Blues have second-placed Arsenal in their sights, but arch rivals Manchester United will take some catching:

Team	P	W	D	L	F	A	Pts
Manchester United	582	367	131	84	1,140	516	1,232
Arsenal	582	308	157	117	974	517	1,081
Chelsea	**582**	**285**	**158**	**139**	**912**	**580**	**1,013**
Liverpool	582	285	144	153	925	579	999
Newcastle United	540	229	142	169	799	653	829

— BULLDOG BRITS AND JOHNNY FOREIGNERS —

On Boxing Day 1999 Chelsea sparked a press storm by becoming the first English club to field a team entirely consisting of overseas players. The Blues side which won 2–1 at Southampton was made up of two Frenchmen (Frank Leboeuf and Didier Deschamps), two Italians (Roberto di Matteo and Gabriele Ambrosetti), a Romanian (Dan Petrescu), a Nigerian (Celesetine Babayaro), a Dutchman (Ed de Goey), a Norwegian (Tore Andre Flo), a Uruguayan (Gus Poyet), a Brazilian (Emerson Thome) and a Spaniard (Albert Ferrer).

The last time Chelsea fielded a team wholly made up of British players was against Leicester City at Filbert Street on 6 May 1995. Even so, one of the players, Mark Stein, had been born in South Africa. The other ten British-born Blues were Kevin Hitchcock, Steve Clarke, Scott Minto, Frank Sinclair, David Lee, Nigel Spackman, Craig Burley, Gavin Peacock, David Hopkin and Paul Furlong.

— CHAMPIONS 'DOUBLED' —

On just two occasions Chelsea have recorded 'doubles' over the season's eventual champions. In 1958/59 the Blues beat Wolves 6–2 at the Bridge and 2–1 at Molinuex. Despite these results, the Midlands club went on to win the league by six points while Chelsea had to settle for 14th place.

More recently, in the 1993/94 season, Chelsea beat 'Double' winners Manchester United home and away. Gavin Peacock was the Blues' hero in both games, scoring the only goal in 1–0 wins at the Bridge and Old Trafford.

— EUROPEAN PARTNERS —

Chelsea have faced opponents from 24 different countries in European competition: Austria, Belgium, Bulgaria, Czech Republic, Denmark, England, France, Germany, Greece, Holland, Israel, Italy, Latvia, Luxembourg, Norway, Portugal, Russia, Scotland, Slovakia, Spain, Sweden, Switzerland, Turkey and Yugoslavia.

The Blues have met Spanish opposition most often (24 games, including a record 11 against Barcelona) followed by encounters with teams from Italy (13 games).

— CHELSEA'S SHORTEST SEASON —

When, in September 1939, Adolph Hitler decided to invade Poland he not only brought an end to the 'Peace in our time' promised by British Prime Minister Neville Chamberlain, but also called a premature halt to the 1939/40 football season.

Like other teams in the First Division, the Blues had played just three games when the Football League season was suspended the day after Britain's formal declaration of war against Germany on September 3. For those of you who are too young to remember or were too busy practicing air-raid drills to care, here are Chelsea's results in full from the truncated season:

Date	Result
August 27 1939	Chelsea 3 Bolton Wanderers 2
August 31 1939	Chelsea 1 Manchester United 1
September 2 1939	Liverpool 1 Chelsea 0

— PLAYER OF THE YEAR —

The Chelsea Player of the Year award was established in 1967, in memory of long-serving chairman Joe Mears who had died the previous year. Since then 30 different players have won the trophy, but only three (John Hollins in 1971, Ray Wilkins in 1977 and Frank Lampard in 2005) have managed to retain it the following year. Wilkins also holds the record as the youngest player to win the award, being just 19 when he first topped the poll in 1976. The oldest winner is the evergreen Gianfranco Zola, who was 37 when he claimed the trophy for a second time in 2003. The full list of winners is as follows:

Year	Player
1967	Peter Bonetti
1968	Charlie Cooke
1969	David Webb
1970	John Hollins
1971	John Hollins
1972	David Webb
1973	Peter Osgood
1974	Gary Locke
1975	Charlie Cooke
1976	Ray Wilkins
1977	Ray Wilkins
1978	Mickey Droy

1979	Tommy Langley
1980	Clive Walker
1981	Petar Borota
1982	Mike Fillery
1983	Joey Jones
1984	Pat Nevin
1985	David Speedie
1986	Eddie Niedzwiecki
1987	Pat Nevin
1988	Tony Dorigo
1989	Graham Roberts
1990	Ken Monkou
1991	Andy Townsend
1992	Paul Elliott
1993	Frank Sinclair
1994	Steve Clarke
1995	Erland Johnsen
1996	Ruud Gullit
1997	Mark Hughes
1998	Dennis Wise
1999	Gianfranco Zola
2000	Dennis Wise
2001	John Terry
2002	Carlo Cudicini
2003	Gianfranco Zola
2004	Frank Lampard
2005	Frank Lampard
2006	John Terry
2007	Michael Essien

— FA CUP FINALS AT THE BRIDGE —

In the years immediately before the construction of Wembley Stadium, Stamford Bridge was the venue for three FA Cup finals (results below). The ground has also hosted ten FA Cup semi-finals, the most recent in 1978 when Arsenal beat Orient 3–0.

Year	FA Cup Final result	Attendance
1920	Aston Villa 1 Huddersfield Town 0	50,018
1921	Tottenham 1 Wolves 0	72,805
1922	Huddersfield Town 1 Preston North End 0	53,000

— THE OTHER STAMFORD BRIDGE —

Confusingly for some, there is a village called Stamford Bridge in Yorkshire which is famous for being the site of the battle in September 1066 in which Harold II of England defeated an invasion by his brother Tostig and Harald III of Norway. A month later Harold had less luck when he came up against another invading force led by Duke William (later William I) at the Battle of Hastings.

Incidentally, Stamford Bridge derives its name from the bridge that spans the railway line alongside the ground, rather than from the battle site.

— UNUSUAL MIDDLE NAMES —

Craig **Lorne** Forrest
Geremi **Sorelle Ndjitap** Fotso
Keith **Aubrey** Jones
Dmitri **Victorvitch** Kharine
Graeme **Pierre** Le Saux
Eddie **John Ikem** Newton
David **Carlyle** Rocastle
Frank **Mohammed** Sinclair
George **Oppong** Weah
Clive **Euclid Aklana** Wilson
Mikael **Kaj** Forssell
Derek **Tennyson** Kevan

— SUCCESSFUL SKIPPERS —

John Terry is the most successful captain in the history of Chelsea. To date, the England defender has lifted five major trophies for the Blues: the Premiership in 2005 and 2006, the Carling Cup in 2005 and 2007 (although, on the latter occasion, Terry had left the pitch injured and cup-collecting duties were passed to Frank Lampard), and the FA Cup also in 2007.

The full list of trophy-winning Chelsea captains is as follows:

Captain	Number of Major Trophies Won
John Terry	5
Dennis Wise	4
Ron Harris	2
Roy Bentley	1
Terry Venables	1

— SIGNED FROM NON-LEAGUE XI —

1. Vic Woodley (from Windsor and Eton, 1931)
2. Darren Barnard (Woking, 1990)
3. Chris Hutchings (Harrow Borough, 1980)
4. Derek Saunders (Walthamstow Avenue, 1953)
5. Mickey Droy (Slough Town, 1970)
6. George Mills (Bromley, 1929)
7. Jim Lewis (Walthamstow Avenue, 1952)
8. Kenny Swain (Wycombe Wanderers, 1973)
9. Seamus O'Connell (Bishop Auckland, 1954)
10. Ian Hutchinson (Cambridge United, 1968)
11. Paul Canoville (Hillingdon Borough, 1982)

— BLACK EASTERS —

In 1959 Chelsea journeyed up to Blackpool at Easter and were hammered 5–0. The following day Ted Drake's team travelled across the Pennines to Leeds and did slightly better, only succumbing 4–0.

Unbelievably, the Blues fared even worse over the same holiday period 27 years later. On Easter Saturday 1986 John Hollins' men were crushed 4–0 at home to West Ham and, two days later, went down to another humiliating defeat, 6–0, on the plastic pitch at Queens Park Rangers. To add to the Blues' woes, striker David Speedie was sent off at Loftus Road.

— DOH! —

During the 1998/99 season the Chelsea matchday programme asked the squad to nominate their favourite characters from *The Simpsons*. Many of the players didn't watch the show, but among the ones who did Homer Simpson was the most popular character:

Marcel Desailly: Homer
Michael Duberry: Homer
Albert Ferrer: Bart
Bjarne Goldbaek: Bart
Bernard Lambourde: Homer/Apu
Jody Morris: Homer
Eddie Newton: Homer
Mark Nicholls: Homer/Maggie
Graeme Le Saux: Homer/Maggie
John Terry: Homer
Gianfranco Zola: Chief Wiggam

— COBHAM TRAINING GROUND —

In December 2004 Chelsea moved from their old, windswept training ground in Harlington to a state-of-the-art facility in Cobham, Surrey. Covering an area of 3,338m sq, the site's features include:

- 15 football pitches
- Three pitches with revolutionary undersoil heating
- One indoor artificial grass pitch for use in winter
- The latest in training and rehabilitation equipment
- Moat around main building to allow light into basement area

— MOST SURPRISING TRANSFER —

Imagine one of Chelsea's top players, Frank Lampard or Arjen Robben for example, leaving the Blues to join a lower division side for a record transfer fee. It just wouldn't happen. Yet, in November 1947, that's precisely the scenario which unfolded when Chelsea's England international Tommy Lawton left the Bridge for Notts County, then in the Third Division (South). The fee, £20,000, was a record for Britain at the time. Despite his drop down the divisions, Lawton continued to be picked for England and finished his international career with the remarkable record of 22 goals in 23 games.

— PACKET OF TEN —

Cough, cough, wheeze, wheeze . . . 'Pass the fags, mate. Cheers!' Not the sort of conversation you'd expect to hear in the Chelsea dressing room these days, but in the past the Blues team has contained more than its share of smokers. A couple of players have owned up to a preference for a somewhat stronger drug, too. Naughty boys.

Player	Drug of choice
Tommy Baldwin	Cigarettes
Alan Birchenall	Menthol cigarettes
William 'Fatty' Foulke	Snuff
Frank Leboeuf	Cigarettes
Eddie McCreadie	Cigarettes
Adrian Mutu	Cocaine
Graham Rix	Cigarillos
Gianluca Vialli	Cigarettes
Walter Winterbottom (wartime guest player)	Pipe

— NAUGHTY BOYS —

During the 2000/01 season the Chelsea matchday programme asked the Blues' squad what was the naughtiest thing they did as a child. Here is a selection of their answers:

Sam Dalla Bona: "I slashed my sofa when I was five or six with a knife. I can't remember why I was so angry. My parents just slapped me and bought another."

Jesper Gronkjaer: "We found some frozen strawberries in the freezer, and started throwing throwing them at a neighbours' door. They had a white wall. Then it became red!"

Eidur Gudjohnsen: "When I was ten or eleven and living in Reykjavik me and a couple of mates broke into our school and sprayed fire extinguishers."

Kevin Hitchcock: "When I used to live in Plaistow as a kid, we used to go to the top of the maisonettes and launch eggs at bus drivers and people getting off buses."

Jes Hogh: "In a cooking class at school my friend threw a wet cloth at me. I caught it and threw it back at him, but he ducked and it hit the teacher in the face. She went mad and threw me out of the class for the rest of the year."

Graeme Le Saux: "I left a fish head in a girl's pencil case once in biology. We were dissecting fish and she wouldn't do it as she didn't like fish. She opened her pencil case in the next lesson, home economics, and found the fish head."

John Terry: "We had a mad geezer on our estate. When he came out, a few of the lads were hiding and egged him and threw flour at him so it stuck. He used to chase us, but he never caught any of us."

Gianfranco Zola: "While my father was loading his lorry, I found a knife and completely cut the seat where I was sitting. The lorry was new and my father was not best pleased."

— DEBUT BOYS —

The greatest number of Chelsea players to make their first-team debut in the same match is 11 for the Second Division game against Stockport County at Edgeley Park on 2 September 1905. The fact that this was the Blues' first ever match helped, of course.

Otherwise, the record stands at nine. Bill Robertson, Danny Winter, Albert Tennant, Robert Russell, John Harris, Reg Williams, Tommy Lawton, Len Goulden and Jimmy Bain all made their Chelsea debuts in the third round (first leg) FA Cup tie at home to Leicester City on

5 January 1946. Again, though, this was a statistical oddity explained by the six-year gap in first-class fixtures during World War II.

In more normal circumstances, the record number of players to make their Chelsea debuts in the same match is six, set on 13 August 2003 against MSK Zilina in the Champions League qualifying round (Wayne Bridge, Glen Johnsen, Geremi, Juan Sebastian Veron, Damien Duff and Joe Cole) and equalled on 15 August 2004 against Manchester United at Stamford Bridge (Petr Cech, Paulo Ferreira, Alexey Smertin, Didier Drogba, Ricardo Carvalho and Mateja Kezman).

— CHATTING WITH ROMAN —

By all accounts, Roman Abramovich's English is pretty limited. Just imagine, then, how thrilled the Chelsea supremo would be to meet a fan who could talk to him in Russian. Here's a step-by-step guide to initiating a simple conversation with Abramovich in his native lingo:

Good afternoon/good evening: Dobri dyen/dobri vyecher
Chelsea are great!: Chelsea – ochen kharosho!
Tottenham are rubbish!: Tottenham – moosar!
Goodbye: Da sveedaneeya

— PLAY-OFF ONE-OFF —

Chelsea are the only side in the modern era to have been relegated from the top flight in a play-off. So-called 'Test' matches were originally used to decide promotion and relegation issues in the 1890s, and were re-introduced as 'play-offs' in 1986/87. The following season Chelsea finished in the play-off position (18th) in the old First Division and had to fight for their survival with three Second Division clubs, Middlesbrough, Blackburn and Bradford City. After beating Blackburn in the semi-final (6–1 on aggregate), the Blues faced Middlesbrough in the final. Following a 2–0 defeat in the first leg at Ayresome Park, Chelsea could only manage a 1–0 win at the Bridge in the return and were relegated. Serious crowd trouble after the match led to the FA ordering the closure of Chelsea's terracing for the first six games of the next season and also resulted in the play-off system being modified to only include clubs attempting to gain promotion.

— STATESIDE BLUES —

In the 1970s football in America experienced a boom, thanks largely to a number of world-class players, including Pele, Franz Beckenbauer and Johan Cruyff, joining NASL teams towards the end of their illustrious careers. Quite a few former Chelsea players hopped across the Atlantic to join them, including this complete team of ex-Blues:

Player	Club(s)
1. Peter Bonetti	St Louis Stars
2. John Boyle	Tampa Bay Rowdies
3. John Dempsey	Philadelphia Furies
4. Garry Stanley	Lauderdale Strikers/ Wichita Wings
5. Alan Hudson	Seattle Sounders
6. Charlie Cooke	Los Angeles Aztecs/ California Surf
7. Keith Weller	New England Tea Men/ Fort Lauderdale Strikers
8. Tommy Baldwin	Seattle Sounders
9. Peter Osgood	Philadelphia Furies
10. Alan Birchenall	San Jose Earthquakes/ Memphis Rogues
11. Clive Walker	Fort Lauderdale Strikers
Manager: Eddie McCreadie	Memphis Rogues

— SING-A-LONG WITH CHELSEA —

The word 'Chelsea' has appeared in quite a few song titles over the years, largely because it's a famous area in both London and New York. Here, in order of artistic merit, is our Top Five . . . enjoy, pop-pickers:

Song title	Artist	Year Released
1 Chelsea Morning	Joni Mitchell	1967
2 (I Don't Want to Go to) Chelsea	Elvis Costello	1978
3 Chelsea Dagger	The Fratellis	2006
4 Chelsea Monday	Marillion	1983
5 Chelsea Girl	Simple Minds	1979

— SHARE AND SHARE ALIKE —

The fewest number of Chelsea players to find the net in a single season is seven in 1938/39. Unsurprisingly, given their shot shy attack, the Blues struggled all through the campaign and only avoided relegation to the old Second Division by a single point. At the end of the season Chelsea fans were indebted to leading scorers Joe Payne (17), George Mills (12) and Dickie Spence (11), without whose goals the drop would have been a formality.

At the other end of the scale, the Blues have on three occasions shared their seasonal haul of goals among no fewer than 18 players. In 2003/04 Jimmy Floyd Hasselbaink (17) and Frank Lampard (15) led the way as Claudio Ranieri's finished second in the league and reached the semi-finals of the Champions League. In 1996/97 Mark Hughes (14) and Gianfranco Zola (12) top scored for Ruud Gullit's FA Cup winners. However, in 1909/10 Jimmy Windridge was the most prolific of the Blues' 18 marksmen with a paltry six goals. The lack of a regular scorer proved to be a fatal problem for Chelsea, who were relegated after finishing 19th in the First Division.

— LIKE FATHER, LIKE SON —

Most Blues fans know that Frank Lampard's dad played for West Ham but the midfielder is not alone among Chelsea players in following in his father's footsteps. Just check out this complete team of past and present Blues, all of whose dads were also pretty good with the ball at their feet:

Player	Father	Father's (main) club
1. Carlo Cudicini	Fabio	AC Milan
2. John Sillett	Charles	Southampton
3. Neil Clement	Dave	QPR
4. Juan Sebastian Veron	Juan snr	Estudiantes
5. Gavin Peacock	Keith	Charlton
6. Ray Wilkins	George	Brentford
7. Frank Lampard	Frank snr	West Ham
8. Eidur Gudjohnsen	Arnor	Anderlecht
9. Kerry Dixon	Mike	Luton
10. Brian Laudrup	Finn	Brondby
11. Clive Allen	Les	Tottenham
Manager: Jose Mourinho	Felix	Vitoria Setubal

— WARTIME GUESTS —

A number of famous names played for Chelsea as guests during the world wars when the Football Association relaxed its normally stringent registration rules. Well-known loan stars appearing at the Bridge included:

World War I: Charles Buchan (the man behind 'Charles Buchan's soccer monthly')
World War II: Walter Winterbottom (future England manager)
Matt Busby (future Manchester United manager)
Joe Mercer (future England manager)
Eddie Hapgood (Arsenal and England)

— HEADS! . . . OR, ER, MAYBE TAILS —

Chelsea's European fate has twice been decided by the toss of a coin. In 1966 the Blues met AC Milan in the third round of the Fairs Cup, the precursor of the UEFA Cup. Milan won the first leg 2–1 before Chelsea triumphed in the second leg at the Bridge by the same score. A play-off match, held in Milan, ended 1–1 after extra-time forcing the tie to be settled by a toss of the coin. Chelsea skipper Ron Harris called correctly and the Blues went through to the next round.

Two years later, in 1968, Chelsea were paired with DWS Amsterdam in the Fairs Cup second round. After two 0–0 draws, the Blues' hopes again relied on Ron Harris' ability to call 'heads' or 'tails' correctly. Sadly, 'Chopper' called incorrectly and the Blues went out.

— YOUNG GUN, OLD STAGER —

The youngest player to have appeared for Chelsea is Ian 'Chico' Hamilton, who made his Blues debut at the age of 16 years, 4 months and 18 days against Tottenham at White Hart Lane on 18 March 1967. He headed Chelsea's equaliser in a 1–1 draw.

The oldest player to have pulled on a Blues shirt is Dickie Spence, who was aged 39, 1 month and 26 days when he made his final appearance for the club in a 1–1 draw against Bolton Wanderers at the Bridge on 13 September 1947.

Graham Rix became Chelsea's oldest debutant when he came on as a substitute at home to Viktoria Zizkov in the European Cup Winners Cup on 15 September 1994 at the age of 36 years, 10 months and 23 days. Rix, who was Chelsea's youth team coach at the time, was called into service because Uefa's 'foreigners rule' restricted clubs to selecting just three non-English players.

— ONE-GOAL WONDERS —

As the saying goes, it only takes a second to score a goal. Sometimes, though, it can take a good deal longer – just look at this list of Chelsea players, all of whom played over 100 games for the club, but who only found the net once for the Blues:

Player	Appearances	Goal	Year
George Barber	294	v Brighton (A)	1933
Erland Johnsen	182	v Southampton (H)	1994
Graham Wilkins	149	v Middlesbrough (H)	1979
Albert Ferrer	113	v Hertha Berlin (H)	1999
John Sillett	102	v Doncaster Rovers (A)	1960
Andrew Ormiston	102	v Leicester Fosse (H)	1912

— BLUES BROTHERS —

Four sets of brothers have played for Chelsea. In chronological order, they are William and Christopher Ferguson (1928); Peter and John Sillett (1957-61); Allan and Ron Harris (1963-67); and Graham and Ray Wilkins (1973-79).

Meanwhile, a number of Chelsea players have had brothers who played professionally for other clubs. These include:

Player	Brother
Celestine Babayaro	Emmanuel (Besiktas)
Ian Britton	Billy (Forfar)
Steve Clarke	Paul (Kilmarnock)
Didier Drogba	Joel (St. Pauli)
Tore Andre Flo	Jostein (Sheffield United)
Glenn Hoddle	Carl (Barnet)
John Hollins	Dave (Newcastle)
Salomon Kalou	Bonaventure (Auxerre)
Ray Lewington	Chris (Wimbledon)
Derek Smethurst	Peter (Blackpool)
Alexey Smertin	Yevgeny (Dynamo Moscow)
Mark Stein	Brian (Luton)
John Terry	Paul (Yeovil Town)
Roy Wegerle	Steve (Feyenoord)
Shaun Wright-Phillips	Bradley (Manchester City)

— JIMMY'S GOAL-FILLED SEASON —

Legendary goal poacher Jimmy Greaves hit a post-war top flight record 41 league goals in the 1960/61 season, including six hat-tricks. The teams to feel the full force of Greavsie's striking powers were Wolves (three goals in a 3–3 draw), Blackburn (three goals in a 5–2 win), Manchester City (three goals in a 6–3 win), West Brom (five goals in a 7–1 win), Newcastle (four goals in a 6–1 win) and, in his last match for the Blues, Nottingham Forest (four goals in a 4–3 win).

— BLUES BLEMISH FOR GOONERS —

As every footy fans knows, Arsenal won the league in 2003/04 without losing a match. The Gunners' championship side of 1990/91 very nearly matched that feat, losing just one game in the 38-match league programme. The team to wipe the smile from the north Londoners' faces, if only temporarily, was Chelsea who beat Arsenal 2–1 at the Bridge on 2 February 1991. Kerry Dixon and rookie striker Graham Stuart scored for the Blues, with Alan Smith hitting a late consolation goal for the champions-elect.

— GRIM CHRISTMAS —

There was little festive cheer for Chelsea fans in 1960 as they saw their team lose 2–1 at home to Manchester United on Christmas Eve. At the time it was customary to play the same team twice in a Yuletide double-header, so on Boxing Day the Blues travelled to Old Trafford where they were on the wrong end of a 6–0 thrashing. The mince pies and Christmas pud tasted no better after the next match, a 6–1 hammering at Wolves on New Year's Eve. Oh well, surely the New Year would bring better luck? Wrong! In their first match of 1961 the Blues crashed out of the FA Cup, losing 2–1 at home to Fourth Division Crewe Alexandra.

— WORLD CUP BLUES —

Chelsea supplied more players to countries competing in the 2006 World Cup than any other club on the planet: 17, two more than nearest rivals Arsenal.

The Blues' previous best tally was 11 players at the 1998 tournament in France. Of this group, Frank Leboeuf and Marcel Desailly went on to become the first Chelsea players to win the World Cup, while Tore Andre Flo, Dan Petrescu and Brian Laudrup all scored, making them the first Chelsea players to get on the scoresheet in the finals.

The full list of World Cup Blues is:

Year	Venue	Players
1950	Brazil	Roy Bentley (England)
1958	Sweden	Peter Brabrook (England)
1966	England	Peter Bonetti (England, unused)
1970	Mexico	Peter Bonetti (England), Peter Osgood (England)
1986	Mexico	Kerry Dixon (England)
1990	Italy	Tony Dorigo (England), Dave Beasant (England, unused)
1994	USA	Erland Johnsen (Norway) Dmitri Kharine (Russia)
1998	France	Celestine Babayaro (Nigeria), Marcel Desailly (France), Albert Ferrer (Spain), Tore Andre Flo (Norway), Ed de Goey (Holland, unused), Brian Laudrup (Denmark), Frank Leboeuf (France), Roberto di Matteo (Italy), Dan Petrescu (Romania), Graeme Le Saux (England), Frank Sinclair (Jamaica)
2002	Japan/Korea	Celestine Babayaro (Nigeria), Marcel Desailly (France), Jesper Gronkjaer (Denmark), Emmanuel Petit (France), Mario Stanic (Croatia)
2006	Germany	Michael Ballack (Germany), Wayne Bridge (England, unused), Ricardo Carvalho (Portugal), Petr Cech (Czech Republic), Joe Cole (England), Hernan Crespo (Argentina), Didier Drogba (Ivory Coast), Michael Essien (Ghana), Paulo Ferreira (Portugal), William Gallas (France), Asier del Horno (Spain)*, Robert Huth (Germany), Frank Lampard (England), Claude Makelele (France), Arjen Robben (Holland). Andriy Shevchenko (Ukraine), John Terry (England)

* Named in the original squad, but withdrew through injury

— KEEPING UP APPEARANCES —

Ron Harris lifts the 1970 FA Cup

Chelsea's all-time leading appearance maker is Ron Harris, who played in an amazing total of 795 games following his debut in February 1962. Nicknamed 'Chopper' because of his no-nonsense approach to defending, Ron was the Blues' skipper when Chelsea won the FA Cup in 1970 and the European Cup Winners' Cup the following year. After seeing off his nearest challenger, team-mate Peter Bonetti, Ron left the Blues to become player/coach at Brentford in the summer of 1980.

The top ten Chelsea appearance makers are:

Player	Years Played	Appearances
1. Ron Harris	1962–80	795
2. Peter Bonetti	1960–79	729
3. John Hollins	1963–84	592
4. Dennis Wise	1990–2001	445
5. Steve Clarke	1987–98	421
6. Kerry Dixon	1983–92	420
7. Eddie McCreadie	1962–73	410
8. John Bumstead	1978–91	409
9. Ken Armstrong	1947–57	402
10. Peter Osgood	1964–79	380

— LIGHTS OUT! —

One of the strangest episodes in Chelsea history occurred on 29 January 1969 when the Blues were playing Preston in an FA Cup fourth round replay at the Bridge. Two goals to the good, Chelsea appeared to be cruising into the next round when, suddenly, the Bridge floodlights failed with 15 minutes still to play. Referee Ken Burns had no option but to call the game off and the match was re-played the following Monday afternoon, Chelsea winning 2–1 thanks to late goals by David Webb and Charlie Cooke. Despite the game being played on a working day the attendance at the Bridge, 36,522, was only 1,000 down on Chelsea's average for the season – presumably thousands of fans phoned in sick or suddenly remembered they had a funeral to go to . . .

— WINNING RUNS —

Chelsea set a new club record by winning nine matches on the trot at the start of the 2005/06 season. The teams swept aside by the Blues were Arsenal (FA Community Shield), Wigan Athletic, Arsenal again, West Bromwich Albion, Tottenham Hotspur, Sunderland, Anderlecht (Champions League), Charlton Athletic and Aston Villa. The run came to an end when Liverpool held Jose Mourinho's men to a 0-0 draw at Anfield in the Champions League.

The Blues had previously won eight consecutive games on three separate occasions: in 1927, 1989 and 2004.

— TOP GOAL GRABBERS —

Chelsea's all-time highest scorer is 1960s star Bobby Tambling. A Chelsea youth product, Bobby scored for the Blues on his debut in a 3–2 win over West Ham at Stamford Bridge in February 1959 . . . and found the net another 201 times over the next decade. His best haul was five goals away to Aston Villa in September 1966.

1980s hotshot Kerry Dixon threatened to overtake Bobby's longstanding record, but a poor last season at the Bridge when he only scored six goals ruined his chances.

Chelsea's all-time highest scorers are:

Player	Goals	Games	Goals/ Games ratio
Bobby Tambling	202	370	0.55
Kerry Dixon	193	420	0.46
Roy Bentley	150	367	0.41
Peter Osgood	150	380	0.39
Jimmy Greaves	132	169	0.78

— BLUE IS THE COLOUR —

To mark their achievement in reaching the League Cup Final in 1972, the glamorous Chelsea team of the period recorded 'Blue is the Colour' at a studio in Islington, north London. Released on Penny Farthing Records the single reached number five in the charts, making it one of the most successful club songs in pop history.

This is how the chart looked in the week Chelsea played Stoke in the League Cup final at Wembley in early March 1972:

1. Nilsson, *Without You*
2. Don MacLean, *American Pie* _
3. Chicory Tip, *Son of my Father*
4. New Seekers, *Beg, Steal or Borrow*
5. Paul Simon, *Mother and Child Reunion*
6. Michael Jackson, *Got To Be There*
7. **Chelsea FC, *Blue is the Colour***
8. Gilbert O'Sullivan, *Alone Again (Naturally)*
9. Lindisfarne, *Meet Me on the Corner*
10. Slade, *Look Wot You Dun*

— ALL WE ARE SAYING IS GIVE US A GOAL! —

The Blues' worst run in front of goal came towards the end of the 1980/81 season, when the team went nine games without finding the net. The dismal run began on 14 March 1981 with a 1–0 defeat at Bristol Rovers and continued until the opening day of the following season when Colin Lee hit the first goal in a 2–0 defeat of Bolton Wanderers at the Bridge on 29 August 1981. In all, 876 minutes had elapsed since the previous Chelsea goal on 7 March 1981 – ironically, also scored against Bolton, this time by Alan Mayes. The nine games in which the Blues failed to score were:

Date	Result
14 March	Bristol Rovers 1 Chelsea 0
21 March	Chelsea 0 Blackburn Rovers 0
28 March	Newcastle 1 Chelsea 0
4 April	Chelsea 0 Cardiff City 1
11 April	Oldham 0 Chelsea 0
18 April	Chelsea 0 Bristol City 0
20 April	Chelsea 0 Luton Town 2
25 April	Swansea City 3 Chelsea 0
2 May	Chelsea 0 Notts County 2

— A CUP'S A CUP —

Over the years Chelsea have won a number of minor cups and trophies. These victories may not have got the fans singing in the streets, but for Blues supporters they were welcome nonetheless:

Year	Competition	Result	Venue
1919	London Victory Cup	Chelsea 3 Fulham 0	Highbury
1945	Football League (South) Cup	Chelsea 2 Millwall 0	Wembley
1951	Festival of Britain Trophy	Chelsea 1 KB Copenhagen 0	Stamford Bridge
1965	Glasgow Charity Cup	Glasgow Select XI 0 Chelsea 3	Hampden Park
1986	Full Members Cup	Chelsea 5 Manchester City 4	Wembley
1990	Zenith Data Systems Cup	Chelsea 1 Middlesbrough 0	Wembley

1993	Cross-Channel Cup	Chelsea 4 Le Havre 2 (agg)	Home/ away
1993	Makita Tournament	Tottenham 0 Chelsea 4	White Hart Lane
1996	Umbro Cup	Chelsea 2 Ajax 0	City Ground
1997	Umbro Cup	Everton 1 Chelsea 3	Goodison Park
2003	Premier League Asia Cup	Chelsea 0 Newcastle 0*	Malaysia
2005	Samsung Cup	Benfica 0 Chelsea 1	Estadio da Luz

* Chelsea won 5–4 on pens

— WEATHER WOES —

- Four Chelsea matches have been abandoned as a result of bad weather. The most recent was on 20 December 1972 when thick fog descended on Carrow Road in the final minutes of the Blues' League Cup semi-final against Norwich, leading ref Gordon Hill no option but to call the game off. With Chelsea trailing 3–2 (and 5–2 on aggregate) this was definitely a lucky break for the Londoners, but it turned out to be merely a stay of execution as the Canaries won the rearranged fixture 1–0 to reach the final.
- On 29 October 1932 the Blues' First Division match against Blackpool at Bloomfield Road went ahead despite a freezing cold wind and sub-zero temperatures – according to the local evening paper: "the worst day climatically for many seasons." In the second half four Chelsea players decided they'd had enough and, living up to their 'southern softies' reputation, rushed off to the warmth of the dressing room. The sturdy northerners remained at full strength and won the match 4–0.

  Remarkably, Chelsea manager David Calderhead kept the same team for the next match, while the club programme also leapt to the defence of the players who walked off: "Those ready to disparage the quitters should know that in each case the player had barely enough strength left to reach the dressing room before collapsing. Common humanity suggested the game should have been abandoned."
- In recent years the worst conditions Chelsea have played in were in Tromso, northern Norway, in October 1997. With heavy snow

falling throughout the second half the pitch markings completely disappeared yet, to Blues boss Ruud Gullit's annoyance, the referee insisted that the match should continue. Tromso won the game, a second round European Cup Winners Cup fixture, 3–2 but were hammered 7–1 in the return leg at the Bridge when the conditions were much more to Chelsea's liking.

— JIMMY'S THREE-GOAL FIRST —

The first Chelsea hat-trick was notched by Jimmy Windridge in a 5–1 victory over Hull City at Stamford Bridge on 11 September 1905. Windridge, who had joined the Blues from Small Heath (later to become Birmingham City) finished the season with an impressive total of 16 goals in just 20 games, but was pipped to be the club's first ever leading scorer by Frank Pearson, who notched 18 goals in 29 games.

— 'FATTY' FOULKE: CHELSEA'S FIRST SUPER-SIZED SUPERSTAR —

William 'Fatty' Foulke

Willie 'Fatty' Foulke, Chelsea's first goalkeeper and captain, was a huge (in every sense of the word) attraction in the early years of the club. A giant of a keeper signed from Sheffield United, Foulke was 6ft 2 inches tall, weighed a massive 22 stone and wore size 12 boots.

His personality was equally out-sized. Opposition strikers who tangled with him risked being grabbed by the collar and thrown into the net, while it wasn't unknown for Foulke to storm off the pitch in a huff if he felt his team-mates weren't performing adequately. His style as a goalkeeper was surprisingly agile, however, as the very first Chelsea programme pointed out to the fans: "In spite of his bulk he possesses all the activity of a cat, combined with the playfulness of a kitten."

In an effort to intimidate the opposition, Chelsea arranged for two small boys to stand behind Foulke's goal to exaggerate his bulk still further. The plan worked as Foulke kept an amazing nine consecutive clean sheets in his one season stay at the Bridge – a club record which stood for 99 years until surpassed by Petr Cech in the 2004/05 season. The boys also proved useful for collecting and returning the ball when it went out of play behind the goal and so, quite accidentally, the role of 'ball boy' was created.

— WORST RESULT EVER —

Chelsea's heaviest ever defeat was an 8–1 thrashing away to Wolves on 26 September 1953. Remarkably, just over 18 months after this black day in the history of the club, an almost unchanged Blues team had been crowned league champions.

Below is a list of Chelsea's worst defeats in a variety of domestic and European competitions. The squeamish may wish to quickly turn over the page:

Year	Competition	Result
1953	Football League	Wolves 8 Chelsea 1
1905	FA Cup	Crystal Palace 7 Chelsea 1
1974	League Cup	Stoke 6 Chelsea 2
1966	Fairs Cup	Barcelona 5 Chelsea 0
2000	Champions League	Barcelona 5 Chelsea 1
1988	Full Members Cup	Swindon Town 4 Chelsea 0
2002	UEFA Cup	Viking Stavanger 4 Chelsea 2
1995	European Cup Winners Cup	Zaragoza 3 Chelsea 0

— KEY DATES IN THE FORMATION OF CHELSEA FC —

28 April 1877: 6,000 people attend the opening of Stamford Bridge, the new home of the London Athletic Club.

29 September 1904: The Mears brothers, Gus and Joseph, take possession of the freehold of Stamford Bridge.

14 March 1905: Fulham FC having turned down the chance to play at Stamford Bridge, the Mears brothers and their colleague Fred Parker decide to form a new club which will apply for league membership.

24 March 1905: The name of the club, Chelsea FC, is chosen in preference to the three other options: Kensington FC, London FC and Stamford Bridge FC.

27 March 1905: John Tait Robertson, a Scottish international half-back, is appointed as player/manager of the new club on a salary of £4 per week.

20 April 1905: Chelsea announce that they are applying for election to the Football League, having received little encouragement from other London clubs for their application to the Southern League.

26–27 April 1905: Chelsea sign their first players: centre-half Bob McRoberts and inside-forwards Jimmy Robertson and Jimmy Windridge. All three arrive from Small Heath (later to become Birmingham City) and the combined fee is just £340. Within the next three weeks another ten players are signed, including 22 stone goalkeeper Willie 'Fatty' Foulke.

29 May 1905: Football League meeting at Tavistock Hotel, Covent Garden. Without having kicked a single ball, Chelsea are elected to the Second Division of the league, along with Leeds City, Hull City and Clapton Orient.

1 September 1905: The Chelsea team travel on the 6.05pm train from Euston to Manchester, ahead of their first ever match at Stockport County. The party stays at the Albion Hotel in Manchester.

2 September 1905: Chelsea's first match in the Second Division ends in a 1–0 defeat.

— MOST UNLIKELY TV APPEARANCE —

Teddy Maybank, an occasional striker at the Bridge between 1975 and 1977, appeared on ITV's Saturday primetime show *Blind Date* some years after leaving Chelsea.

— FOREIGN LEGION STALWARTS —

Six overseas players have made more than 200 appearances for Chelsea and they are:

Gianfranco Zola (1996–2003)	312 apps
Eidur Gudjohnsen (2000–2006)	263 apps
William Gallas (2001–2006)	225 apps
Marcel Desailly (1998–2004)	222 apps
Dan Petrescu (1995–2000)	208 apps
Frank Leboeuf (1996–2001)	204 apps

— OUR SHEETS ARE CLEAN . . . —

Chelsea goalkeeper Petr Cech set an English top flight record in 2004/05 by clocking up 1,024 Premiership minutes without conceding a goal. This incredible run fell just 39 minutes of the all-time English record, set by Reading keeper Steve Death in 1979. Cech's ten consecutive shut-outs during this period – against Norwich (4–0), Aston Villa (1–0), Portsmouth (2–0), Liverpool (1–0), Middlesbrough (2–0), Tottenham (2–0), Portsmouth (3–0), Blackburn (1–0), Manchester City (0–0) and Everton (1–0) – broke the longstanding club record of nine clean sheets set by Willie 'Fatty' Foulke in season 1905/06 and, more importantly, helped Chelsea consolidate their position at the top of the Premier League.

— . . . AND NOT SO CLEAN —

In season 1960/61 the Blues managed just one clean sheet in 42 league games, a young Peter Bonetti denying the Preston strikers in a 2–0 Chelsea win at Deepdale. The Blues ended the campaign having conceded a club record 100 goals; there was better news at the other end, however, where Jimmy Greaves and co. scored 98 goals – also a club record.

— CHELSEA HOTSPURS —

Chelsea and Tottenham may be fierce London rivals, but that didn't stop the players in this team from spending time at both Stamford Bridge and White Hart Lane:

1. Neil Sullivan (Chelsea, 2003–04)
2. Colin Lee (1980–87)
3. Clive Wilson (1987–90)
4. Terry Venables (1960–66)
5. Jason Cundy (1990–92)
6. Graham Roberts (1988–90)
7. Mick Hazard (1985–89)
8. Clive Allen (1991–92)
9. Gordon Durie (1985–91)
10. Jimmy Greaves (1957–61)
11. Gus Poyet (1997–2001)
Manager: Glenn Hoddle (1993–96)

— ALBERT'S LONG WAIT —

Albert Tennant signed professional terms with Chelsea in November 1934 but, amazingly, didn't make his first-team debut until 12 years later. Before the war Tennant only played reserve team football for the Blues, while the wartime matches he played in for the club don't count as official games. So, it wasn't until January 1946 that Tennant became a fully-fledged Blue when he appeared in the FA Cup against Leicester City at Stamford Bridge.

— ACCESSORISED KIT —

Perhaps reflecting the quirky nature of the club, a number of Chelsea players have given their team kit an individual twist:

Tom Priestly: to hide his completely bald pate, the 1930s left-winger always wore a brown skull cap during games.

Alan Hudson: in an era before the wearing of shin pads became compulsory, the 70s hero often played with his socks down by his ankles.

Dmitri Kharine: the Blues' Russian keeper always wore black tracksuit trousers, which he felt gave better protection to an old knee injury.

Roberto di Matteo: the Italian midfielder was the first player to wear his socks pulled up above his knees, a style since copied by Thierry Henry.

William Gallas, Marcel Desailly, Celestine Babayaro and Gianfranco Zola: when the temperature dropped this quartet could be relied upon to turn out in black gloves.

John Terry: wore a thick white headband for the 2002 FA Cup semi-final against Fulham, after having stitches put in a head wound suffered the previous weekend.

— CLOCKING UP THE AIR MILES —

Between 1969 and 1974 Chelsea visited all five of the world's continents on a series of impossibly exotic summer tours. From their base in Europe, the Blues travelled to:

Africa (Mozambique), 1969
America (Venezuela, El Salvador and Barbados), 1970, 1971 and 1972
Asia (Iran), 1973
Australasia (Australia), 1974

— MYSTERY OF THE WEATHER VANE —

In the early 1930's a weather vane, depicting a player said to be George Hilsdon, was put up on Chelsea's original East Stand. Over time a superstition developed among some fans that Chelsea's fortunes would plummet if the weather vane was ever taken down.

However, in 1972 the weather vane had to be removed when the old East Stand was demolished. Weather-beaten and rusty the vane was sent for extensive repairs to a specialist ironworks in the Midlands. Predictably, according to some at least, Chelsea immediately entered a dark period of financial chaos, falling crowds, rampant hooliganism and depressing results culminating in relegation to the Second Division. The curse of the missing vane had struck.

Even the ironworks, where the model of Hilsdon lay rusting in a pile of scrap, went bankrupt. When Ken Bates became Chelsea chairman in 1982 he was told of the curse and swiftly ordered a new vane to take the place of the original. This was promptly restored to the top of the old West Stand and, within a short time, the Blues' fortunes took a distinct turn for the better, with the club gaining promotion back to the First Division in 1984.

— BIG BLUE CHEESES —

Chelsea have had just ten chairmen since the club was founded in 1905. They are:

1905–35	W. Claude Kirby
1935–36	C.J. Pratt snr
1936–40	Colonel C.D. Crisp
1940–66	J.H. Mears
1966–68	C.J. Pratt jnr
1968–69	L.R. Withey
1969–81	J. Brian Mears
1981–82	Viscount Chelsea
1982–2004	Kenneth W. Bates
2004–	Bruce Buck

— FAMOUS LAST WORDS —

Often hard-hitting, frequently controversial, the Ken Bates column in the Chelsea matchday programme was essential reading for fans between 1982 and 2004. The column appeared for the last time for the home match against Birmingham City on 18 January 2004. Typically, Bates signed off in forthright style, his final paragraph reading:

"Smokers in the West Stand lower, be warned. If you do smoke you will be thrown out. Not by your kind friendly usual steward. We have hired a special hit squad to try and solve this problem. Don't say I didn't tell you." And, no, there wasn't even a cheery 'Enjoy the game!' at the end of that last Bates blast.

— BOO BOY TARGETS —

While most Chelsea players have enjoyed a good relationship with the Stamford Bridge crowd, a handful have suffered from barracking from a section of supporters. Players to be on the wrong end of the boo boys' taunts include:

Peter Houseman (1963–75): the left winger, dubbed 'Mary' by some fans, lacked the glamour possessed by some of his team-mates, while occasional rumours that the iconic George Best was set to join Chelsea from Manchester United didn't help his cause.

Graham Wilkins (1972–82): a loyal Chelsea servant for a decade, Graham was nonetheless compared unfavourably to his much more illustrious brother, Ray. An unfortunate series of own goals didn't do much to endear him to the fans, either.

Paul Canoville (1982–86): a pacy left-winger who contributed some valuable goals in the Blues' 1983/84 promotion campaign, Canoville was disgracefully booed by some fans simply for being black.

Darren Wood (1984–89): a versatile player who could do a job in both defence or midfield, Wood became a target for the terrace snipers when he was picked ahead of the more flamboyant and creative Mick Hazard.

Dave Beasant (1989–92): initially hailed as 'England's Number One', the fans turned on Beasant after a series of high profile boobs cost Chelsea dearly.

Slavisa Jokanovic (2000–02): a methodical but somewhat ponderous midfielder, Claudio Ranieri's first signing never won over the fans and by the end of his stay in West London the simple announcement of Jokanovic's name could be guaranteed to generate a resounding chorus of boos.

— SUPERSUB FLO —

Tore Andre Flo, Chelsea's beanstalk Norwegian striker of the late 1990s, holds the club record for the most goals by a player coming off the bench. In all, Tore hit 12 goals for the Blues in 69 appearances as a sub, adding to the 38 goals he managed as a starter.

Mikael Forssell is another player with an excellent record as a substitute. In January 2002 the Finn scored in four consecutive games – against Bolton, Norwich, West Ham and Tottenham – after coming off the bench each time. Almost as impressively, his total playing time during the four matches was just 89 minutes. In the whole of the 2001/02 season Forssell scored nine goals for the Blues as a sub, setting another club record.

— CHELSEA PLAYERS OR MANAGERS APPEARING IN TV ADVERTS —

Scott Parker: McDonalds (1994)
Ruud Gullit: M & Ms (1996), Pizza Hut (1998)
Terry Venables: British Telecom (1996), Oasis (1997), The Sun (2000)
Ray Wilkins (voice over): Tango (1996)
Glenn Hoddle: Shredded Wheat (1996), The Sun (1998)
Frank Lampard: Sainsbury's (2004)
Jose Mourinho: American Express (2005)
Arjen Robben: Adidas (2005)
John Terry: Pro Evolution Soccer (2006), King of Shaves (2006)

— 10–GOAL THRILLERS —

Chelsea and West Ham fans enjoyed a pre-Christmas treat on 17 December 1966 when they watched their teams share 10 goals in a remarkable 5–5 draw at Stamford Bridge. On target for the Blues in the crazy goal-fest were Tommy Baldwin, Tony Hateley, Charlie Cooke and Bobby Tambling (2).

The only other occasion the Blues have been involved in a 5–5 draw was on 30 October 1937 in a match against Bolton at Burnden Park, inside forward Jimmy Argue hitting a hat-trick for the Londoners. The 38,171 fans who turned up at Stamford Bridge for the return fixture between the clubs later in the season must have been smacking their lips in anticipation of another goal-filled afternoon. Sadly, they were disappointed as the match finished in a 0–0 draw.

— ENGLAND AT THE BRIDGE —

Four full England internationals have been played at Stamford Bridge, the home side winning all of the games. Forget the new Wembley, perhaps England should set up home at the Bridge:

Year	Result
1913	England 1 Scotland 0
1929	England 6 Wales 0
1932	England 4 Austria 3
1946	England 4 Switzerland 1

— WILL WE WIN AGAIN? —

In season 1987/88 Chelsea went 21 league games without a win, the worst such run in the club's history. The dismal sequence began on 3 November 1987 with a 3–1 defeat away to Arsenal and continued until 9 April 1988 when a Mickey Hazard goal gave the Blues all three points at home to Derby County. The record-breaking run cost manager John Hollins his job and was largely responsible for the Blues' ultimate fate – relegation to the Second Division after a play-off defeat by Middlesbrough.

— WHO THE BLEEDIN' HELL ARE YOU? —

Some unlikely figures have pulled on the famous Blues shirt over the years, including:

- Scouse comedian (and Liverpool fan) Jimmy Tarbuck came on as a substitute for Alan Birchenall in Ken Shellito's testimonial against QPR at Stamford Bridge on 6 May 1968. History doesn't record how the tubby comic fared, but Chelsea manager Dave Sexton was clearly insufficiently impressed to sign Tarby up for the following season.
- Ten years later, on 27 November 1978, fans in the Shed were rubbing their eyes with disbelief when Capital Radio DJs Dave Cash and Graham Dene played the second half for Chelsea against QPR. OK, it was only another testimonial game – this time for Blues long-throw legend and 1970 FA Cup winner Ian Hutchinson – but Rangers seemed to be taking the game somewhat more seriously . . . their two subs were England internationals Ian Gillard and Clive Allen!

- The manager of the Chelsea restaurant, Leon Lenik, swapped his dinner jacket for a football shirt to come on as a substitute for Colin Pates in Mickey Droy's testimonial match against Arsenal at Stamford Bridge on 1 November 1983. The Blues won the game 2–1, with Droy scoring one of the home team's goals.
- On 14 May 1984 Chelsea programme editor Hugh Hastings replaced Kerry Dixon in a testimonial match for Brentford's Eddie Lyons at Griffin Park. Hastings, it has to be said, didn't quite live up to the standard set by Dixon who had scored five goals by the time he was substituted. Chelsea won the match 6–3.
- Another non-footballer to get a run out for the Blues is former Chelsea masseur and diehard fan Terry Byrne. Terry came on for Frank Leboeuf towards the end of the Blues' 6–0 tour match defeat of Brunei in May 1997 and, by all accounts, acquitted himself well. Nonetheless, then boss Ruud Gullit resisted the temptation to promote him to the first-team squad.
- Finally, fitness trainer Antonio Pintus replaced Bjarne Goldbaek for the last five minutes of the Blues' match against Instant District of Hong Kong in May 1999. Chelsea won the game 2–1.

— GOING UP! —

Chelsea have won promotion to the old First Division on seven occasions, winning the Second Division championship twice. The matches which confirmed the Blues' rise into the top flight are listed below:

Year	Result	Matches left	Final position	Also promoted
1907	Chelsea 4 Wolves 0	2	2nd	Nottm Forest
1912	Chelsea 1 Bradford Park Ave 0	-	2nd	Derby County
1930	Bury 1 Chelsea 0	-	2nd	Blackpool
1963	Chelsea 7 Portsmouth 0	-	2nd	Stoke City
1977	Wolves 1 Chelsea 1	1	2nd	Wolves, Nottm Forest
1984	Chelsea 5 Leeds 0	3	1st	Sheff Weds, Newcastle
1989	Chelsea 1 Leeds 0	3	1st	Man City, Crystal Palace

— DERBY DELIGHT . . . AND MISERY —

There are few sights Chelsea supporters enjoy more than watching the Blues give a right old pasting to one of their London rivals. Conversely, just thinking about those occasions when Chelsea have experienced a derby drubbing can still bring some Blues fans out in a cold sweat years later. Here, then, are Chelsea's best and worst ever results against the other main London teams – those of a delicate disposition may wish to cover up the scores on the right-hand side . . .

Club	Best result	Worst Result
Arsenal	Arsenal 0 Chelsea 5 (1998)	Chelsea 1 Arsenal 5 (1930)
Charlton	Chelsea 5 Charlton 0 (1962)	Charlton 4 Chelsea 0 (1977)
Fulham	Chelsea 4 Fulham 0 (1925, 1984)	Fulham 3 Chelsea 0 (1951)
QPR	QPR 0 Chelsea 4 (1968)	QPR 6 Chelsea 0 (1986)
Tottenham	Tottenham 1 Chelsea 6 (1997)	Tottenham 5 Chelsea 0 (1920)
West Ham	Chelsea 6 West Ham 2 (1966)	West Ham 4 Chelsea 0 (1981) Chelsea 0 West Ham 4 (1986)

— THE SAYINGS OF JOSE MOURINHO —

"We have top players and, sorry if I'm arrogant, we have a top manager. Please don't call me arrogant, but I'm European champion and I think I'm a special one."

Shortly after being appointed Chelsea manager, July 2004

"My philosophy in football is that there is only one winner. The second is the first of the last."

Revealing his ultra-competitive streak, July 2004

"As we say in Portugal, they bought the bus and they left the bus in front of the goal."

After Tottenham had packed their defence to gain a 0–0 draw at the Bridge, September 2004

"I think I'm a special one."

"Maybe when I turn 60 and have been managing in the same league for 20 years I'll have the respect of everybody, I'll have the power to speak to people and make them tremble a bit."
Accusing Sir Alex Ferguson of influencing the referee, January 2005

"In football, top people are never scared. We always want to play against the big teams, the big managers; players always want to play big players."
**After the Champions League draw paired Chelsea with Barcelona,
December 2004**

"Defeat in the first leg is not a defeat. We are just losing at half-time."
**Looking on the bright side, before the Champions League last 16
second leg with Barcelona, March 2005**

"What honeymoon? The only honeymoon I have had is the 20 years
with my wife."
**Responding to the question 'Is the honeymoon over?'
after two defeats on the trot, February 2005**

"I'm feeling a lot of pressure with the problem in Scotland. Football
is nothing compared with life. For me bird flu is the drama of the last
few days. I'll have to buy a mask."
**More worried about bird flu than Manchester United's ultimately
futile title challenge, April 2006**

"Don't talk to me about cricket. I don't understand the game. You
have to wait three days to see who wins!"
Revealing that he is not a fan of the summer game, August 2006

"I think it would be difficult for anyone to be manager of any club
after me. I wouldn't recommend it."
Fully aware that he's a tough act to follow, January 2007

"If I believe what I read in the press there are already 11 candidates
for my job. Even if the lists in the media become even bigger it's still
no problem for me. I'm very happy."
Remaining cool under pressure, January 2007

"You show when you are happy, you show when you are not happy.
Sometimes you kiss (the players), sometimes you kick."
On his management style, January 2007

"There are only two ways for me to leave Chelsea. One is in June
2010, when I finish my contract. If the club does not give me a new
one it is the end of my contract and I am out. The second way is for
Chelsea to sack me because there's not a third way."
**Denying reports that he might leave Chelsea of his own accord,
February 2007**

"Who am I to question the owner of the club? Abramovich is all-
powerful at Chelsea."
**Acknowledging his subordinate position in Chelsea's hierarchy,
March 2007**

— 2004/05: A RECORD-BREAKING SEASON —

Chelsea's championship-winning side of 2004/05 not only won the title at a canter but also set a number of significant top flight, Premiership and club records, including:

- The Blues' total of 95 points is an all-time top flight record. Manchester United previously held the record with 92 points in their first 'Double' season, 1993/94.
- Chelsea's goals against tally of just 15 equalled Preston's record, set in the Football League's first season, 1888/89. However, Preston only played 22 games and the previous record for fewest goals conceded in a League campaign was usually previously credited to Liverpool (16 goals conceded in 42 games in 1978/79).
- In the second half of the season Chelsea won nine consecutive away league games, setting a new top flight record for English football. The run only ended on the final day of the campaign when the Blues were held to a 1–1 draw at Newcastle.
- During the 2004/05 season the Blues recorded 10 consecutive clean sheets in the Premiership, setting another all-time top flight record. The previous best of eight was jointly held by Liverpool (1922/23) and Arsenal (1998/99).
- Eight consecutive Premiership wins all with clean sheets equalled an all-time European top flight record held jointly by Partizan Belgrade and Skonto Riga.
- Chelsea's total of 25 clean sheets in the League set a new Premiership record, surpassing Manchester United's 24 in 1994/95. However, Liverpool retain the all-time top flight record with 28 clean sheets in 1978/79.
- Chelsea's record of just one league defeat in a league campaign is a club record and has only ever been surpassed in the top flight by Preston (1888/89) and Arsenal (2003/04), both of whom went through a whole league season unbeaten.
- The Blues' goal difference of +57 was the best in the club's history, beating the previous best of +53 set in 1905/06.
- Throughout the 2004/05 season Chelsea suffered just six defeats, equalling a club record established in 1998/99. The only sides to beat Mourinho's Blues were Manchester City (Premiership), Newcastle (FA Cup) and Porto, Barcelona, Bayern Munich and Liverpool in the Champions League.
- 12 league doubles – against Manchester United, Everton, Liverpool, Middlesbrough, Charlton, Blackburn, Portsmouth, Fulham, West Bromwich Albion, Crystal Palace, Norwich and

- Southampton – created a new club record, beating the eight the Blues managed in 1906/07 and 1962/63.
- Goalkeeper Petr Cech set a new club record of 28 clean sheets, beating Ed de Goey's previous record of 27 in season 1999/2000. Altogether, Chelsea recorded 34 clean sheets, another club record.
- The Blues' total of 15 away league victories set a new club record, beating the previous best of 14 in the old Second Division in 1988/89.
- Chelsea's total of 42 games won in all competitions set yet another club record, beating the previous best of 36 wins in 2003/04.

— 16–GOAL EXTRAVAGANZA —

On 29 November 1966 Chelsea played a London XI, featuring such legendary names as Bobby Robson, Johnny Haynes and England World Cup winner George Cohen, in a testimonial match for the Blues' long-serving defender John Mortimore. The final score was 9–7 to Chelsea, making this the highest-scoring match the Blues have ever been involved in. The 16 strikes were neatly divided between the first and second halves, and worked out on average at a goal every five minutes and 37 seconds.

— MUSIC INDUSTRY SOCCER SIX —

Between 1999 and 2002 the Music Industry Soccer Six tournament was played at Stamford Bridge, attracting a stellar cast of actors, musicians and ex-footballers and crowds around the 15,000 mark.

The finalists in the four years the competition was held at the Bridge were:

	Winners	Runners-up
1999	Fat Les	Robbie Williams
2000	Robbie Williams	Ant and Dec
2001	Ant and Dec	Rod Stewart
2002	Westlife	Ant and Dec

— CHELSEA UP, TOTTENHAM DOWN —

Blues fans had smiles as wide as the Grand Canyon in May 1977 when Chelsea were promoted to the First Division while hated rivals Tottenham moved in the opposite direction, slipping into the Second Division for the first time since 1950. However, Spurs bounced back the following season and have maintained their top flight status ever since; Chelsea, on the other hand, have suffered two subsequent relegations.

— OUCH! THAT HURT —

A number of Chelsea players have collected injuries in unusual circumstances. These include:

- **John Boyle:** The Blues' midfielder was knocked unconscious when he was struck by a bottle thrown by a Roma fan during Chelsea's Fairs Cup match with the Italians in Rome on October 6 1965. However, Boyle, a tough Scotsman, recovered to play on in the match which ended in a 0-0 draw.

- **Alan Hudson:** The teenage prodigy missed the 1970 FA Cup final after injuring his ankle in a freak incident during a game at West Brom. "There was nobody near me when it happened," he said later. "I just landed badly, my foot went down a hole and that was it. I knew as soon as it happened that it was serious because I was in unbelievable pain." In an effort to get fit for the Blues' Wembley showdown with Leeds, Huddy visited a spiritualist in Victoria. "It was like a palm reading, only she 'read' the bottom of my foot," he recalled. "I was just laughing while she did it and thinking, 'This ain't gonna work'." He was right – it didn't.

- **Steve Kember:** Midfielder Steve had already damaged his front teeth when he was kicked in the face by Ron 'Chopper' Harris while playing against the Blues for Crystal Palace in 1971. He moved to Chelsea later the same year and in 1973 suffered a second unintentional whack in the face from another Blues player. "Playing for Chelsea against Leeds, I went round Paul Madeley one side and Peter Osgood went round him the other," he recalled. "As I've gone to tackle Madeley, Ossie accidentally kicked me in the face and knocked my teeth out again." Painful.

- **Dave Beasant:** In the summer of 1993 goalkeeper Dave was making lunch at home when he knocked a bottle of salad cream off the kitchen work surface. Attempting to prevent the bottle smashing on the floor, Beasant tried to control it with his foot but only succeeded in rupturing ligaments in his ankle. He was sidelined for two months, and didn't play another match for the Blues before joining Southampton.

- **Carlo Cudicini:** The Italian goalkeeper injured himself while taking his dog for a walk in the summer of 2001 and was eventually forced to have minor surgery on his knee. "I don't know whether his dog is a Rottweiler or a Pekinese," Chelsea assistant manager Gwyn Williams told reporters, "but Carlo was out walking it and it must have seen a rabbit or something because it gave him a sharp tug. Carlo felt his knee tweak. He thought it was alright but, a bit later, it was still giving him problems." The bizarre injury kept Cudicini out of the Blues' team until the autumn, although he recovered sufficiently to win the club's Player of the Year award by the end of the campaign.

— TWO FEMALE FIRSTS —

Sharon Rivers made history on 5 December 1994 when she became the first woman to officiate in a match at Stamford Bridge, running the line in an FA Youth Cup second round replay between Chelsea and Leyton Orient. Maybe the young Blues, who included future first team players Jody Morris and Mark Nicholls, found her presence distracting as they lost the match 2–0.

In 1989 Yvonne Todd became the first female member of the board of directors of Chelsea FC. She served on the board until 2003.

— MONEY TOO TIGHT TO MENTION —

Between July 1974, when David Hay arrived from Celtic for £225,000, and September 1978, when the Blues bought Duncan McKenzie from Everton for £165,000, Chelsea did not spend a penny on player purchases. This four-year unofficial 'transfer embargo' was a product of the massive debts - £3.4 million at one point - the club accumulated following the building of the East Stand. With no money to spend on transfer fees, Chelsea instead had to rely on its youth system – so much so that of the 20 players used during the 1976/77 promotion season no fewer than 15 were former members of the youth team. Remarkably, in four games of that same season the eleven players Chelsea fielded had not cost the club a single penny in transfer fees.

— TIME WARP —

On 27 December 1986 Chelsea fans were stunned to discover that, according to the front cover of the matchday programme at least, that afternoon's home game against Aston Villa was taking place on 'Saturday 27th December 1968'. It was just a misprint, of course, but happily the Blues – struggling at the foot of the First Division at the time – showed some of their goal-filled 60s form by thrashing Villa 4–1.

CHELSEA
Home Kits
1874-2008

www.historicalkits.co.uk

1905-09

1909-10

1910-24

1926-27

1934-35

1936-46

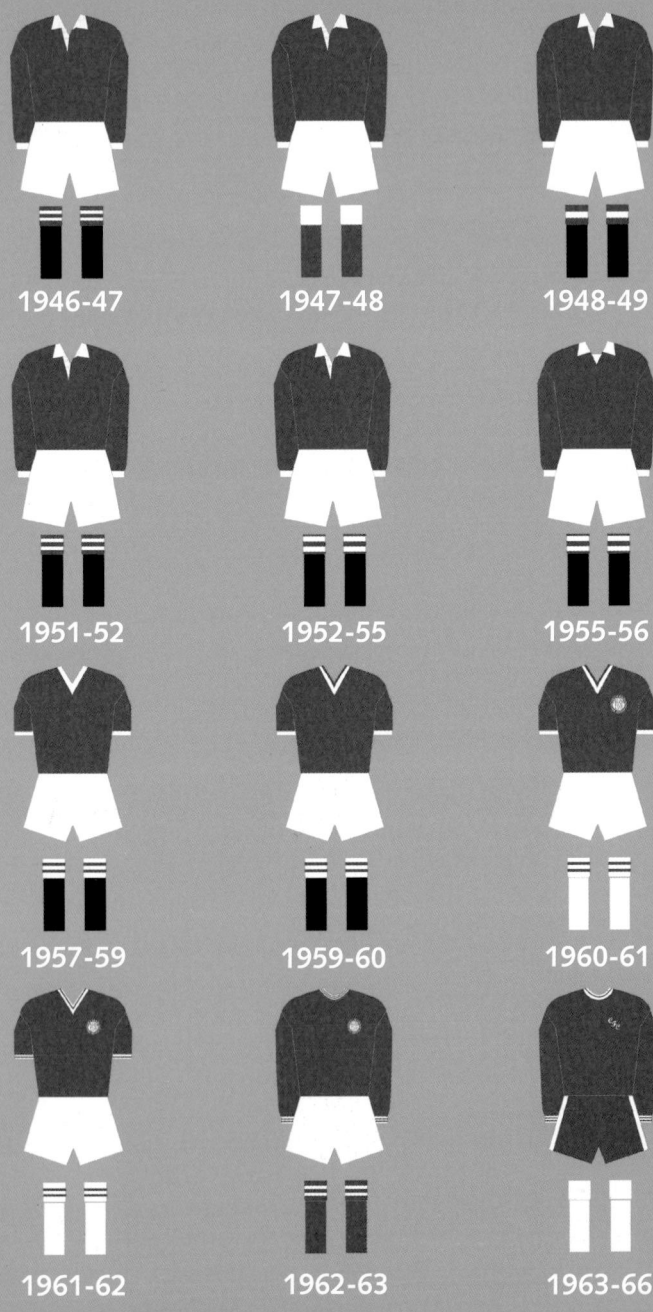

1946-47

1947-48

1948-49

1951-52

1952-55

1955-56

1957-59

1959-60

1960-61

1961-62

1962-63

1963-66

1966-67

1968-70

1970-71

1971-73

1973-74

1975-78

1978-81

1981-83

1983-84

1984-85

1985-86

1986-87

1987-89

1989-91

1991-93

1993-94

1994-95

1995-97

1997-99

1999-2001

2001-03

2003-05

2005-06

2006-08

— SPECIAL GOAL —

Roberto di Matteo scores after 43 seconds

In 2004 the official Chelsea magazine asked readers to vote for the most important goal in the club's history. Once the votes had been added up, the top five goals were:

1) Roberto di Matteo, v Middlesbrough, 1997 FA Cup Final   33%
2) Jesper Gronkjaer, v Liverpool, Premiership 2003   19%
3) David Webb, v Leeds United, 1970 FA Cup Final replay   18%
4) Mark Hughes, v Vicenza, 1998 ECWC semi-final second leg   9%
5) Wayne Bridge, v Arsenal, 2004 Champions League, quarter-final   8%

— A TV RECORD —

The 1970 FA Cup Final replay between Chelsea and Leeds at Old Trafford attracted the largest ever television audience for a domestic match, with more than 28 million viewers tuning in to the live coverage on the BBC and ITV channels. Incredibly, the combined audience figure for the match puts it in the all-time top 10 of British TV ratings successes:

1. World Cup Final (1966)	32.3 million
2. Princess Diana's funeral (1997)	32.1 million
3. EastEnders (Den and Ange divorce episode, 1986)	31.15 million
4. Royal Family documentary (1969)	30.69 million
5. Apollo 13 splashdown (1970)	28.6 million
6. Chelsea v Leeds, FA Cup Final replay (1970)	**28.49 million**
7. Charles and Diana wedding (1981)	28.4 million
8. Princess Anne's wedding (1973)	27.6 million
9. Coronation Street (Blackpool tram horror episode, 1989)	26.93 million
10. Royal Variety Show (1965)	24.2 million

— CHELSEA MANAGERS —

Jose Mourinho is Chelsea's 23rd manager and easily the club's most successful. To date, 'the Special One' has won five major trophies and one minor one in just three years at the Bridge. A number of other managers have fared significantly less well, but none as poorly as Danny Blanchflower who won just five matches in a nine-month spell at the club in the late seventies.

Manager	Years	Trophies Won
John Tait Robertson	1905–06	-
William Lewis	1906–07	-
David Calderhead	1907–33	-
Leslie Knighton	1933–39	-
Billy Birrell	1939–52	-
Ted Drake	1952–61	League Championship (1955), Charity Shield (1955)
Tommy Docherty	1961–67	League Cup (1965)
Dave Sexton	1967–74	FA Cup (1970), European Cup Winners Cup (1971)
Ron Suart	1974–75	-
Eddie McCreadie	1975–77	-
Ken Shellito	1977–78	-
Danny Blanchflower	1978–79	-
Geoff Hurst	1979–81	-
John Neal	1981–85	Second Division Championship (1984)
John Hollins	1985–88	Full Members Cup (1986)
Bobby Campbell	1988–91	Second Division Championship (1989), ZDS Cup (1990)
Ian Porterfield	1991–93	-
David Webb	1993	-
Glenn Hoddle	1993–96	-
Ruud Gullit	1996–98	FA Cup (1997)
Gianluca Vialli	1998–2000	Coca-Cola Cup (1998), European Cup Winners Cup (1998), European Super Cup (1998), FA Cup (2000), Charity Shield (2000)
Claudio Ranieri	2000–04	-
Jose Mourinho	2004–	Carling Cup (2005, 2007), Premiership (2005, 2006) Community Shield (2005) FA Cup (2007)

— TWO TV FIRSTS —

- These days Chelsea feature in more live TV matches than just about any English team. But that wasn't always the case. Indeed, it wasn't until May 1984 that the Blues first appeared in a live league game, the BBC covering their visit to Manchester City in the old Second Division. Chelsea delighted their armchair fans by winning the match 2–0, the goals coming from Pat Nevin and Kerry Dixon.
- The first Chelsea Premiership match to be shown live on Sky was the Blues' visit to Manchester City (again) on Sunday 20 September 1992. The game didn't quite live up to Sky's 'Super Sunday' hype, but Chelsea fans were more than pleased with a 1–0 win thanks to Mick Harford's goal.

— LET THERE BE LIGHT —

The first match to be staged under floodlights at Stamford Bridge was a friendly against Czech side Sparta Prague on 19 March 1957. Six floodlights (a number only matched at the time by Hull City), each 170 feet high, and costing a total of £37,000 illuminated proceedings as the Blues won 2–0 with goals by Les Allen and Derek Gibbs. The experiment was a success with the fans, too, attracting a crowd of 30,701 to the Bridge.

— POMPEY PURPLE PATCH —

The Premiership team the Blues enjoy playing most is Portsmouth. It's now 47 years since Pompey last beat Chelsea (1-0 in a League Cup tie in December 1960). Since then the Pompey chimes have been distinctly muted, as in 22 meetings between the sides in all competitions, the Blues have notched up 16 wins and six draws, scoring 53 goals and conceding just 14.

— BLUE TAXI —

Hail a black cab in London and the chances are that the driver will be an ex-Chelsea player. Among the former Blues to have passed 'the Knowledge' are Gary Chivers, John Bumstead, Alan Dickens, Trevor Aylott and Mickey Hazard. No doubt, the lads would appreciate a decent tip if you do happen to make use of their services.

— DARLING, YOU WERE MARVELLOUS! —

Partly because of Stamford Bridge's location a short distance away from the West End, Chelsea have always been popular among showbiz types. In the 1960s and 1970s famous names such as Sean Connery, Michael Caine, John Cleese, Tom Courtneay, Michael Crawford and Dennis Waterman were regular visitors to the Bridge, while American superstars Raquel Welch and Steve McQueen also saw the Blues in action. Veteran luvvie Lord (Richard) Attenborough, of course, has a long association with Chelsea and is now the club's Life Vice President, having previously been a director.

Actors who regularly attend Chelsea matches these days include Clive Mantle, Phil Daniels and Trevor Eve.

— POINT OF ORDER, MR REFEREE! —

Chelsea enjoy good support on both sides of the House in the Commons and the Lords. Former or current politicians who follow the Blues include:

Sir John Major	(Former Conservative Prime Minister)
David Mellor	(Former Conservative MP for Putney)
Sebastian Coe	(Former Conservative MP for Falmouth and Cambourne, now Lord Coe of Ranmore)
Peter Bottomley	(Conservative MP for Worthing West)
George Osbourne	(Conservative MP for Tatton and Shadow Chancellor)
Peter Hain	(Secretary of State for Wales and Northern Ireland and Labour MP for Neath)

— CUP WINNING BOSSES —

In the early 1990s Chelsea had a trio of managers who shared one thing in common: they had all scored winning goals in the FA Cup Final. Ian Porterfield (manager from 1991–93) had scored Sunderland's winner when they beat Leeds in the 1973 final, while caretaker boss Dave Webb (1993) had, of course, clinched victory for the Blues, again over Leeds, in 1970. Webb's replacement, Glenn Hoddle (1993–96), was another Wembley hero having scored the winner for Spurs in the FA Cup final replay against QPR in 1982. The unusual sequence ended when Ruud Gullit took over from Hoddle in 1996, although he ended up leading the Blues to FA Cup final glory the following year.

— WHAT'S IN A NAME? STAMFORD BRIDGE —

The name of Chelsea's ground derives from a couple of local features and not, as some assume, from the battle of 1066. A stream called Stanford Creek used to run along the route of the present day railway line behind the East Stand, while a bridge called Stanbridge (from 'stone bridge') lay over a creek on the King's Road. It appears that the names of the stream and the bridge evolved into 'Stanford Bridge' and this name was given to the bridge spanning the railway by the main entrance to the ground. At some point, 'Stanford' became 'Stamford' – hence the ground's name.

— SMALL SQUAD PAYS DIVIDENDS —

In 1970 Chelsea used just 13 players during their successful FA Cup run (compared to 18 in 1997 and 22 in 2000). Of these, seven players – Peter Bonetti, John Dempsey, John Hollins, Peter Houseman, Ian Hutchinson, Eddie McCreadie and David Webb – were on the field for all 910 minutes of Cup football. Skipper Ron Harris also started all eight FA Cup games but, feeling the effects of an injury, was substituted at the start of extra-time against Leeds in the final at Wembley.

— GEORGE'S GLORIOUS GOAL —

On 12 January 2000 former World Player of the year George Weah made a dramatic entrance on to the Chelsea scene, coming off the bench to score a late winner for the Blues against London rivals Tottenham. In just a matter of minutes he had become a cult hero for the Bridge fans, and the latest in a short line of players to have scored on their Chelsea debuts as a substitute. Here's the full list:

Year	Player	Player Replaced	Result
1980	Chris Hutchings	Mike Fillery	Cardiff 0 Chelsea 1
1988	David Lee	Darren Wood	Chelsea 2 Leicester 1
1991	Joe Allon	Kevin Wilson	Chelsea 2 Wimbledon 2
1992	Eddie Newton	Graeme Le Saux	Everton 2 Chelsea 1
1997	Paul Hughes	Dennis Wise	Chelsea 3 Derby 1
1997	Tore Andre Flo	Mark Hughes	Coventry 3 Chelsea 2
2000	George Weah	Gus Poyet	Chelsea 1 Tottenham 0

— JIMMY'S QUICK-FIRE HAT-TRICK —

Goal grabber extraordinaire Jimmy Floyd Hasselbaink is the only Chelsea player to have scored a hat-trick after coming on as a sub. Jimmy notched his three goals in a 13–minute spell in the 5–2 defeat of Wolves at Stamford Bridge on 27 March 2004.

Meanwhile, nine players have scored two goals in a match as a sub for the Blues and they are:

Year	Player	Player Replaced	Result
1966	Tommy Baldwin	Peter Houseman	Chelsea 3 Tottenham 0
1985	Paul Canoville	Colin Lee	Sheff Weds 4 Chelsea 4
1998	Gianluca Vialli	Tore Andre Flo	Chelsea 3 Manchester Utd 5
1998	Mark Nicholls	Danny Granville	Chelsea 3 Coventry City 1
1998	Tore Andre Flo	Gianluca Vialli	Chelsea 6 Crystal Palace 2
1998	Tore Andre Flo	Pierluigi Casiraghi	Blackburn 3 Chelsea 4
2001	Gus Poyet	Eidur Gudjohnsen	Derby 0 Chelsea 4
2003	Hernan Crespo	Jimmy Floyd Hasselbaink	Wolves 0 Chelsea 5
2005	Mateja Kezman	Eidur Gudjohnsen	Chelsea 4 Crystal Palace 1
2006	Joe Cole	Lassana Diarra	Chelsea 3 Colchester 1

— WHO'S IN GOAL THIS WEEK? —

Chelsea boss Ruud Gullit helped to set a club record in season 1996/97 by selecting no fewer than five different goalkeepers at one time or another during the campaign. Norwegian international keeper Frode Grodas headed the list with 26 and one sub appearances, followed by Kevin Hitchcock (10 and two sub), Dmitri Kharine (5), on loan goalie Craig Forrest (2 and one sub) and Nick Colgan (one appearance). Presumably, though, Gullit was not especially impressed by any of the quintet as in the summer of 1997 he splashed out £2.25 million to bring Dutch international keeper Ed de Goey to Stamford Bridge.

— CUP WINNERS ALL —

A team of Chelsea players who won the FA Cup with a club other than the Blues:

1. Vic Woodley (Derby County, 1946)
2. Vinnie Jones (Wimbledon, 1988)
3. Asley Cole (Arsenal, 2002, 2003 and 2005)
4. Ray Wilkins (Manchester United, 1983)
5. Graham Roberts (Tottenham, 1981 and 1982)
6. Graham Stuart (Everton, 1995)
7. Jim McCalliog (Southampton, 1976)
8. George Graham (Arsenal, 1971)
9. Jimmy Greaves (Tottenham, 1962 and 1967)
10. Harold Halse (Manchester United, 1909)
11. John Sissons (West Ham United, 1964)

Manager: Ian Porterfield (Sunderland, 1973)

— SPONSORED KIT —

In an effort to raise much-needed revenue Chelsea introduced a kit sponsorship scheme in the 1982–83 season. The idea was that fans or businesses would sponsor an individual player's kit in return for a mention in the club programme. Among the players to be backed in this fashion were:

Player	Kit sponsor
Gary Chivers	Charter Litho Studio Ltd
Phil Driver	Janitorial Management Ltd
Mickey Droy	Fairfax Bookbinders Ltd
Joey Jones	Hotel Lily, Lillie Road SW6
Colin Lee	Rosemary and Ricky Lampton
Colin Pates	'A Season Ticket Holder'
David Speedie	Speedy Cables (London) Ltd
Clive Walker	Laurie Inman

— AWAYDAY BLUES —

1993 was a grim year to follow Chelsea away from home as, incredibly, the Blues failed to record a single victory on opposition soil during the whole calendar year. In all, the Blues played 24 away matches in 1993, losing 16 and drawing eight. The depressing run finally came to an end on New Year's Day 1994 when Chelsea won 3–1 at manager Glenn Hoddle's old club, Swindon Town.

— BEN'S SPECIAL GOAL —

Benjamin Howard Baker holds a unique position in Chelsea history as the only goalkeeper to have scored a goal for the club. His moment of glory came at Stamford Bridge on 19 November 1921 when he slotted a penalty past his Bradford City counterpart Jock Ewart for the only goal of the game. Sadly, Ben's penalty-taking antics soon came to an end when he missed the next one against Arsenal and had to race back in a desperate panic to his own penalty area.

Although not counting as official matches, two Chelsea goalkeepers have scored in testimonial games at the Bridge. In April 1969 Blues legend Peter Bonetti netted two penalties against Charlton in Bobby Tambling's testimonial. 26 years later, in March 1995, Dave Beasant came on for Kerry Dixon in the latter's testimonial match against Spurs and scored the final goal in the Blues' 5–1 win.

— LEAGUE CUP SUCCESS —

The Blues have won the League Cup on four occasions, most recently in 2007 when two Didier Drogba goals saw off Arsenal at the Millennium Stadium in Cardiff. Two years earlier Drogba was on target again as Chelsea defeated Liverpool in the final at the same venue.

The first time the Blues won the competition, in 1965, the final was played over two-legs. After a rare Eddie McCreadie goal secured a 3–2 victory over Leicester at the Bridge, the Blues hung on for a 0–0 draw in the return to take the cup. After a 33–year wait, Chelsea won the League Cup for a second time, extra-time goals from Frank Sinclair and Roberto di Matteo seeing off First Division opponents Middlesbrough.

League Cup Final	Result	Venue
1965	Chelsea 3	Home/
	Leicester City 2 (agg)	away
1972	Chelsea 1 Stoke City 2	Wembley
1998 (Coca-Cola Cup)	Chelsea 2 Middlesbrough 0*	Wembley
2005 (Carling Cup)	Chelsea 3 Liverpool 2*	Millennium Stadium
2007 (Carling Cup)	Chelsea 2 Arsenal 1	Millennium Stadium

* After extra-time

— HOLLY AND FRANKIE'S RECORD RUNS —

Chelsea midfielder John Hollins set a club record in the early 1970s when he appeared in 168 consecutive matches for the Blues. The sequence – which consisted of 135 league games, 10 FA Cup, 19 League Cup and four in the European Cup Winners Cup – began on 14 August 1971 and continued until 25 September 1974.

In season 2005/06 Frank Lampard set a new record for consecutive appearances in the Premiership. When his run came to an end through illness in December 2005 Lampard's total stood on 164, five ahead of David James' previous Premiership record of 159.

Frank Lampard, 164 games in a row!

— PREMIERSHIP CHAMPIONS 2005 —

In season 2004/05 the Blues won their first Premiership title, exactly 50 years after their last championship triumph in 1955. As well as the glory, Chelsea pocketed £9.5 million in prize money for coming first. Here's how the top of the Premiership table looked at the end of the campaign:

	P	W	D	L	F	A	Pts
Chelsea	38	29	8	1	72	15	95
Arsenal	38	25	8	5	87	36	83
Manchester United	38	22	11	5	58	26	77

— GOALKEEPING CRISIS AVERTED —

On two occasions Chelsea have had to play the full 90 minutes with an outfield player in goal and, miraculously, both stand-ins somehow managed to keep a clean sheet. In Chelsea's very first season defender Bob Mackie filled in for regular keeper Willy 'Fatty' Foulke on 28 October 1905 and helped the Blues win 1–0 away to Southern United in the FA Cup.

On 27 December 1971 occasional emergency keeper David Webb donned the green jersey for the visit of Bobby Robson's Ipswich Town, after injuries ruled out Peter Bonetti and John Phillips and third choice goalkeeper Steve Sherwood failed to arrive at the Bridge in time for kick off. Having knelt down and prayed in front of the Chelsea fans in the Shed, Webb then proceeded to keep the Ipswich strikers at bay for the whole game as Chelsea ran out 2–0 winners.

Other outfield players to have pulled on the gloves for Chelsea for part of a game include Bert Murray, Bill Garner, Tommy Langley, David Speedie, John Coady, Vinnie Jones, Glen Johnson and, most recently, John Terry.

— BLUE PUNDITS —

Watch a live football match on the TV or tune into a commentary on the radio and there's a good chance that the former or current pro footballer analysing the game will be a former Chelsea player. Ex-Blues earning a crust in the punditry game currently include:

Clive Allen (ITV)
Craig Burley (Radio Five Live)
Tony Cascarino (Talksport)
Jason Cundy (Talksport)
Kerry Dixon (Smooth FM)
George Graham (Sky TV)
Tommy Langley (Chelsea TV)
Pat Nevin (Channel Five)
Gavin Peacock (BBC TV and Radio Five Live)
Graham Stuart (Smooth FM)
Andy Townsend (ITV and Talksport)
Terry Venables (ITV)
Gianluca Vialli (Sky Italia)
Clive Walker (Radio London)
Ray Wilkins (Sky TV)

— STAMFORD BRIDGE: A POTTED HISTORY —

Stamford Bridge has been the home of Chelsea FC since the club was formed in 1905, although the stadium itself dates back to 1877. Over the decades the ground has radically changed in appearance, and now bears no relation to the stadium fans knew as recently as the early 1970s. What hasn't changed, though, is the sense among Chelsea supporters that Stamford Bridge is their much-loved ancestral home. Here are the key dates in the evolution of the stadium:

1877 Stamford Bridge opens to the public as the home of the London Athletic Club.

1904 The Mears brothers, Gus and Joseph, purchase the freehold of the stadium with a view to using it to stage sporting events, including football.

1905 The 5,000 capacity original East Stand is built, along with vast new terraces. Chelsea FC plays its first competitive match at the Bridge, beating Hull City 5–1.

1935 The Shed is erected above the terraces at the Fulham Road End.

1939 The original North Stand, with a capacity of 2,500, is built above the terraces in the north-east corner of the ground.

1966 The original West Stand opens to fans. Built at a cost of £150,000, it consists of 6,300 seats in 35 rows and, at the front, 3,360 bench seats.

1974 The 11,000–capacity East Stand opens, having cost £2 million. Original plans to make it the first phase of a new 60,000 all-seater stadium are shelved.

1975 The North Stand is demolished.

1994 The Shed End terrace is demolished and replaced with a small temporary stand. Later the same year the North Stand (now the Matthew Harding Stand) opens with a capacity of 10,776.

1997 The West Stand is demolished and the new Shed Stand opens.

2001 After a delay of two years due to planning permission not being granted by the local council, the completed West Stand opens. Built at a cost of around £30 million, it can seat 13,500 fans. In total, the redeveloped Stamford Bridge has a capacity of 42,522. In addition, the stadium complex boosts two four-star hotels, five restaurants, conference and banqueting facilities, a nightclub, an underground car park and a health club.

— MANY MILES FROM HOME —

Chelsea's 1,550–mile trek from London to Moscow for the 2004 Champions League match away to CSKA Moscow is the furthest the Blues have travelled to play a competitive game.

Yet that encounter seems almost like a local derby compared to the tour game the Blues played in Hobart, Tasmania in June 1965 – the island off the south-east coast of Australia is over 11,000 miles from London.

— TRANSFER MILESTONES —

Apart from a spell in the 1970s when the club was stoney broke, Chelsea have never been shy about splashing the cash in the transfer market. Here are some milestones along the way to the Blues' current most expensive purchase, Andriy Shevchenko.

Year	Player	Fee	Selling Club
1907	Fred Rouse	£1,000	Stoke City
1923	Andy Wilson	£5,000	Middlesbrough
1930	Hughie Gallacher	£10,000	Newcastle United
1966	Tony Hateley	£100,000	Aston Villa
1990	Andy Townsend	£1.2 million	Norwich City
1997	Graeme Le Saux	£5 million	Blackburn
1999	Chris Sutton	£10 million	Blackburn
2005	Michael Essien	£24.4 million	Lyon
2006	Andriy Shevchenko	£30.8 million	AC Milan

— ALBERT SQUARE BLUES —

The Queen Vic in *EastEnders* may be something of a West Ham pub (no wonder the regulars are all so gloomy!) but, in real life, Albert Square boasts a fair few Chelsea supporters, including:

Actor	Character
Gemma Bissex	Clare Bates (step-daughter of fat Nigel)
Charlie Brooks	Janine Butcher (scheming daughter of Frank)
Phil Daniels	Kevin Wicks (car salesman)
Michael Greco	Beppe di Marco (nightclub barman)
Michael Higgs	Andy Hunter (gangland bookie)
Martine McCutcheon	Tiffany Raymond (tragic heroine)
Alison Parteger	Sarah Cairns (knife-wielding stalker)
David Spinx	Keith Miller (TV addict layabout)
Daniella Westbrook	Sam Mitchell (original incarnation)

— GIANT-KILLED! —

In recent seasons it has generally taken the big guns – especially Arsenal and Manchester United – to knock Chelsea out of the two domestic cup competitions. That hasn't always been the case, though, and over the years the Blues have been unceremoniously dumped out of either the FA Cup or League Cup by numerous small fry. Here are ten of the worst cup upsets the Londoners have suffered:

Year	Competition	Opponent's Division	Result
1905	FA Cup	Southern League	Crystal Palace 7 Chelsea 1
1914	FA Cup	Southern League	Chelsea 0 Millwall 1
1933	FA Cup	Div 3 (South)	Brighton 2 Chelsea 1
1935	FA Cup	Div 3 (South)	Luton 2 Chelsea 0
1958	FA Cup	Div 3 (North)	Darlington 4 Chelsea 1*
1961	FA Cup	Div 4	Chelsea 1 Crewe 2
1975	League Cup	Div 4	Crewe 1 Chelsea 0
1980	FA Cup	Div 4	Chelsea 0 Wigan 1
1988	League Cup	Div 4	Scunthorpe 4 Chelsea 1 (agg 6–3)
1989	League Cup	Div 4	Scarborough 3 Chelsea 2 (agg 4–3)
1990	FA Cup	Div 3	Bristol City 3 Chelsea 1

* After extra-time

— MEN WITH THE MAGIC SPONGE —

Known originally as the 'trainer', many of Chelsea's chief physios have been remarkably long-serving – as you can see from this list:

1905–07	Jimmy Miller
1907–10	Harry Ransom
1910–14	Mr Wright
1919–39	Jack Whitley
1939–46	Arthur Stollery
1946–53	Norman Smith
1953–60	Jack Oxberry
1960–73	Harry Medhurst
1973–88	Norman Medhurst
1988–95	Bob Ward
1995–2005	Mike Banks
2005–07	Dean Kenneally
2007–	Dave Hancock

— BLUE SUNDAY —

Chelsea appeared in the first ever First Division match to be played on a Sunday, losing 1–0 away to Stoke on 27 January 1974. For many years prior to this Football League teams were prohibited from playing on Sundays, and were only given a special dispensation in 1974 because a national fuel crisis (caused by the miners' strike in the winter of 1973/74) meant clubs were not allowed to play under floodlights.

— ROMAN ABRAMOVICH: A POTTED BIOGRAPHY —

- Abramovich was born on 24 October 1966 in Saratov on the Volga River, southern Russia. His mother died of blood poisoning when he just 18 months old and when he was four years old his father was killed in a construction accident. Adopted by his uncle, Abramovich lived for a while in Moscow, then moved to his grandparents' home in the northern region of Komi.
- He studied at the local industrial institute then transferred to Moscow's Gulkin Institute of Oil and Gas, where he sold retread car tyres as a money-spinning sideline.
- After a spell doing national service in the Soviet army, Abramovich concentrated on a business career, trading oil products out of Russia's largest refinery in Ornsk, western Siberia. His entrepreneurial talents were spotted by Boris Berezovsky, Russia's leading tycoon, and together the pair gained a controlling interest in Sibneft, the country's main oil company.
- When Berezovsky went into exile Abramovich became the most important figure at Sibneft. He eventually sold his share in the company to the Russian government controlled Gazprom for £7.4 billion in 2005.
- In July 2003 Abramovich agreed a deal with then Chelsea chairman Ken Bates to buy his majority shareholding in the club, while also underwriting the significant debts built up by Chelsea Village. He immediately bankrolled a spending spree by then manager Claudio Ranieri to the tune of £100 million.
- Abramovich, who in 2007 divorced his second wife Irina with whom he has five children, enjoys a lifestyle befitting a man who, according to the *Sunday Times* rich list, is the second wealthiest person in Britain (behind steel magnate Lakshmi Mittal). He has a home in London, a 440–acre site in Sussex, owns three yachts (including the £72 million Pelorus, formerly owned by Saudi billionaire Al Sheik Modhassan) and a private Boeing 737 jet.

— LONG THROW EXPERTS —

In the late 1930s Chelsea became the first side to use the long throw as a dangerous attacking weapon, thanks to the extraordinary ability of left-half Sam Weaver to hurl the ball deep into the opposition penalty area. According to newspaper reports of the time, some of his throws even reached the far post - a distance few long throw experts have managed since.

Weaver, though, is remembered less often than Ian Hutchinson, who famously created the Blues' winner in the 1970 FA Cup Final replay with a trademark mega-throw into the Leeds penalty box. 'Hutch' was something of a freak of nature, being double-jointed in both shoulders – an accident of birth which allowed him to send the ball soaring through the sky in a whirl of rotating arms. Little wonder, then, that when Chelsea won a throw in the final third of the pitch commentators would often describe it as being "as good as a corner."

— TREBLES ALL ROUND —

Prior to the start of the 2007/08 season, the last ten Chelsea players to score hat-tricks were:

Year	Player	Result
2007	Frank Lampard	Chelsea 6 Macclesfield 1
2006	Didier Drogba	Chelsea 4 Watford 0
2006	Didier Drogba	Levski Sofia 1 Chelsea 3
2004	Eidur Gudjohnsen	Chelsea 4 Blackburn 0
2004	Jimmy Floyd Hasselbaink	Chelsea 5 Wolves 2
2002	Jimmy Floyd Hasselbaink	Chelsea 4 Tottenham 0
2000	Jimmy Floyd Hasselbaink (4)	Chelsea 6 Coventry City 1
2000	Gus Poyet	Hull City 1 Chelsea 6
1998	Gianluca Vialli	Chelsea 4 Aston Villa 1
1997	Tore Andre Flo	Tottenham 1 Chelsea 6

— AUSSIE BLUES —

As anyone who has ever glanced at an Australian pools coupon knows there is a Chelsea FC down under. Hailing from Melbourne, and with a largely ex-pat Croatian fanbase the team takes its name from a local suburb and has no connection with the 'real' Chelsea.

— TEAM OF THE CENTURY —

In 2005, Blues fans were invited to vote for their greatest ever Chelsea team on the club's official website, www.chelseafc.com. 49 different players were nominated but, once the votes were all counted, the team chosen by the supporters and unveiled at a Centenary dinner at Stamford Bridge in August 2005 looked like this:

Peter Bonetti

Steve Clarke   Marcel Desailly   John Terry   Graeme Le Saux

Dennis Wise   Frank Lampard   Charlie Cooke

Gianfranco Zola

Peter Osgood   Bobby Tambling

— SPORTING ALL-ROUNDERS —

A handful of Chelsea players have excelled in other sports, and they include:

- England international **Max Woosnam** (1914) won four 'blues' at Cambridge and went on to play Davis Cup tennis for Great Britain.
- Goalkeeper **Benjamin Howard Baker** (1921-25) competed in the high jump event at the Olympic Games in 1912 and 1920. A fine tennis player, he also appeared at Wimbledon in the All-England Lawn Tennis championship.
- **John Jackson** (1933–39) was a Scottish international goalkeeper who later became a professional golfer.
- **Clive Walker** (1977–84) was a top sprinter as a schoolboy in Oxford, and once recorded a time of time of 11.2 seconds in a 100m race at Stamford Bridge – not bad, especially as he was wearing football boots!
- **Paul Williams** (1983) made just one appearance for the Blues, against Oldham in April 1983, and then competed in the London Marathon the following week.
- **Nigel Spackman** (1983–87 and 1992–96) represented Hampshire at cross-country as a schoolboy.
- Since retiring from football, **Roy Wegerle** (1986–88) has competed in a number of professional golf tournaments.

- When he was 16, **Michael Duberry** (1994–98) came second for England in the Home Nations triple jump.
- **Bolo Zenden** (2001–04) practiced judo for 12 years in his native Holland and is a black belt.
- **Wayne Bridge** (2003–) represented Hampshire as a sprinter when he was young, recording a best time for the 100m of 11.2 seconds.

— TWO-TIME BLUES —

A handful of players have found the lure of Stamford Bridge so irresistible they have returned to Chelsea for a second spell at the club:

Player	Year transferred	Year returned
Bob Whittingham	1914 (to South Shields)	1919 (from Stoke City)
Alec Cheyne	1932 (to Nimes)	1934 (from Nimes)
Ron Greenwood	1945 (to Bradford Park Avenue)	1952 (from Brentford)
Allan Harris	1964 (to Coventry)	1966 (from Coventry)
Charlie Cooke	1972 (to Crystal Palace)	1975 (from Crystal Palace)
Peter Osgood	1974 (to Southampton)	1979 (from Philadelphia Furies)
Alan Hudson	1974 (to Stoke City)	1983 (from Seattle Sounders)
Peter Bonetti	1975 (to St. Louis Stars)	1975 (from St. Louis Stars)
John Hollins	1975 (to QPR)	1983 (from Arsenal)
Steve Wicks	1979 (to Derby)	1986 (from QPR)
Nigel Spackman	1987 (to Liverpool)	1992 (from Glasgow Rangers)
Ken Monkou	1992 (to Southampton)	2002 (out of contract)
Graeme Le Saux	1993 (to Blackburn)	1997 (from Blackburn)

— . . . AND THE FAN WHO RETURNED TO THE FOLD —

David Mellor was a regular at the Bridge in the 1970s but, around the time when he became MP for Putney in 1979, transferred his affections to Fulham. When Chelsea's fortunes took an upturn during the mid-80s, Mellor switched back to his first love and – despite the Cottagers' unexpected rise to the Premiership – has remained faithful to the Chelsea cause ever since.

— NON-SCORING STRIKERS —

Chelsea have made an unfortunate habit of splashing out big money on forwards who subsequently fail to live up to expectations. The prototype misfiring striker was the Blues' first £100,000 signing, Tony Hateley, although his tally of six goals in 27 league games was positively Greaves-like compared to the desperate goals/games and pounds spent ratios of some of his successors.

Heading the list of striking flops is Chris Sutton. Chelsea's first £10 million player endured a miserable season at the Bridge in 1999/2000, notching just one Premiership goal all year. Unsurprisingly, at the end of the campaign he was swiftly sold off to Celtic for a substantial loss.

'Striker'	Transfer fee	Premiership Games*	Goals	Games/ Goals	£/ Goals
Chris Sutton	£10m	28	1	28	£10 m
Pierluigi Casiraghi	£5.4m	10	1	10	£5.4m
Mateja Kezman	£5m	25	4	6.25	£1.25m
Robert Fleck	£2.1m	38	3	12.66	£700,000

* including substitute appearances

— THE £10,000 GOAL —

At the start of the 2005/06 season Chelsea set a new top flight record by going six league games at the start of the season without conceding a single goal. With the Blues threatening to run away with the Premiership, *The Sun* newspaper decided to up the stakes by offering a £10,000 cash prize to the first opposition player to breach Chelsea's watertight defence. In the 43rd minute of the seventh game of the season Aston Villa's Luke Moore claimed the money when he struck the ball past Petr Cech – unfortunately for the young striker, under the terms of *The Sun's* offer, he had to donate the hefty cheque to charity.

— SHORT, BUT NOT SO SWEET —

Of the 51 players who have made just one appearance for Chelsea, a number have endured nightmare matches:

- Goalkeeper Stanley Macintosh conceded six goals in a 6–2 thrashing at Derby on 6 December 1930.

- Rookie keeper Les Fridge fared little better, letting in five on his first and last appearance at home to Watford on 5 May 1986. Chelsea lost the game 5–1. Michael Pinner also conceded five goals in his only appearance for the Blues, a 5–4 home defeat by Wolves on 20 April 1962.
- Centre-half Frank Wolff and right-winger James Toomer played their only games for the Blues in a 7–1 defeat by Crystal Palace in the FA Cup on 18 November 1905. The Chelsea side was essentially a reserve team as a league fixture was scheduled for the same day.
- Former Morton players Billy Sinclair and Jim Smart both made one-off appearances for the Blues at Burnley in a 6–2 defeat on 24 April 1965. Again, Chelsea fielded a severely weakened team as manager Tommy Docherty had sent eight first-team players home for a breach of club discipline during their stay at a Blackpool hotel.
- More recently, Joel Kitamirike's one game for the Blues was the desperately disappointing 2–0 Uefa Cup defeat away to Hapoel Tel Aviv on 1 November 2001. The young defender was called up for the first team after a number of established players, including Marcel Desailly, Emmanuel Petit and Graeme Le Saux, chose not to travel to Israel at a time of local and international tension.

— CHELSEA CRICKETERS —

In the past it was quite common for footballers to play professional cricket during the summer. Like most clubs, Chelsea have fielded a number of players who were also handy with bat and ball:

Jimmy Windridge (1905–10) played football for England and cricket for Warwickshire.

Willy 'Fatty' Foulke (1905–06) was Chelsea's first ever goalkeeper and played four times for Derbyshire.

Joe Payne (1938–46) played Minor Counties cricket for Bedfordshire.

Frank Mitchell (1949–52) made 17 first-class appearances for Warwickshire.

Ron Tindall (1955–61) made over 170 appearances for Surrey.

Ron Harris (1962–80) was a batsman/wicketkeeper on the groundstaff at Lords but turned down the chance to become a cricketer, choosing to sign for Chelsea instead.

Geoff Hurst (manager 1979-81) made a handful of appearances for Essex.

— NOW, WHICH WAY ARE WE KICKING, AGAIN? —

In a bizarre match played at Stamford Bridge between Chelsea and Swindon Town on 11 February 1989 three of the five goals scored were own goals. Swindon's Jonathan Gittens and Ross MacLaren helpfully netted for the Blues, while Joe McLaughlin got on the scoresheet for the visitors. Chelsea won the match 3–2, with all the goals coming in the first half.

— CHELSEA ACROSS THE POND —

Chelsea is a popular name for towns, villages and districts in the United States. Here are six of them:

Chelsea, Alabama (population, 2,949)
Chelsea, Maine (pop, 2,559)
Chelsea, Massachusetts (pop, 35,080)
Chelsea, Michigan (pop, 4,398)
Chelsea, Oklahoma (pop, 2,136)
Chelsea, Vermont (pop, 1,250)

— A SHED-LOAD OF SMITHS —

Seven men called Smith have played for Chelsea, making this the most common surname among Blues players in the club's history.

- Philip Smith made just one appearance for the Blues, in a 1–0 defeat away to Bristol city on April 16 1910.
- Full-back George Smith made 370 appearances for the club between 1921 and 1930.
- Half-back Stephen Smith made his debut two days after George in 1921, but only went on to make a total of 23 appearances for the Blues.
- Welsh full-back Jack Smith made his debut in 1938, but his Chelsea career was cut short by the outbreak of World War II.
- Striker Bobby Smith scored 30 goals for Chelsea in 86 games in the 1950s and went on to figure in Tottenham's 1961 Double-winning team.
- Left-winger Jimmy Smith was a bit-part player on the Bridge scene during the early 1950s.
- Youth product Jimmy Smith made his debut as a sub against Newcastle in the final match of the 2005/06 season.

— THE EX FACTOR —

Since the Premiership began in 1992 nine Chelsea players have scored against one or other of their former clubs in the league. They are:

Date	Player	Result
12 Sept 1992	Andy Townsend	Chelsea 2 Norwich City 3
12 April 1993	Dennis Wise	Chelsea 4 Wimbledon 2
25 Aug 1993	Gavin Peacock	Chelsea 2 QPR 0
10 Sept 1994	Gavin Peacock	Newcastle 4 Chelsea 2
21 Oct 1995	Mark Hughes	Chelsea 1 Manchester United 4
24 Sept 1997	Mark Hughes	Manchester United 2 Chelsea 2
20 Dec 1997	Dan Petrescu	Sheffield Wednesday 1 Chelsea 4
23 Dec 2001	Eidur Gudjohnsen	Chelsea 5 Bolton Wanderers 1
12 Jan 2002	Eidur Gudjohnsen	Bolton Wanderers 2 Chelsea 2
1 Jan 2003	Emmanuel Petit	Arsenal 3 Chelsea 2
23 Oct 2004	Damien Duff	Chelsea 4 Blackburn Rovers 0
15 Oct 2005	Eidur Gudjohnsen	Chelsea 5 Bolton Wanderers 1
2 Jan 2006	Frank Lampard	West Ham 1 Chelsea 3

— CHELSEA BEST NICKNAMES XI —

1. The Cat (Peter Bonetti)
2. Chopper (Ron Harris)
3. Jamaica (Paul Elliott)
4. Butch (Ray Wilkins)
5. The Rock (Marcel Desailly)
6. The Wall (Emerson Thome)
7. The Rabbit (Eric Parsons)
8. The Sponge (Tommy Baldwin)
9. The Wig (Kerry Dixon)
10. Jukebox (Gordon Durie)
11. The Rat (Dennis Wise)
    Manager: The Doc (Tommy Docherty)

— CHELSEA HOST BRIDGE PARTIES —

Apart from Chelsea's victories in 1955, 2005 and 2006, Stamford Bridge has been the venue for league title celebrations on three other occasions. Unfortunately, those enjoying the party were the players and fans of the opposition:

- On 22 April 1933 Arsenal clinched the title at the Bridge with a 3–1 victory in front of a huge crowd of 72,260.
- The following year the Gunners returned to SW6 with the title in their sights. This time a 2–2 draw was sufficient to get the Gunners' champagne corks popping.
- On 3 May 1986 Liverpool pipped local rivals Everton for the title after a single goal by Kenny Dalglish gave the Reds victory over Chelsea at Stamford Bridge.

— THE PRICE IS RIGHT? —

As at other football grounds, the cost of admission to Stamford Bridge has soared over the years. The price of the matchday programme (an essential purchase for many fans) has also increased, but not by the same level - as you can see by comparing these figures:

	Terraces~	Cheapest reserved seat~	Programme
1970	30p	60p	5p
1975	50p	80p	10p
1980	£2	£3	35p
1985	£3	£6	60p
1990	£6/£7*	£10/£12*	£1.30
1995	£9/£10*^	£11/£15*	£2
2000	N/A	£25/£30*	£3
2005	N/A	£43	£3

*Price depending on match category
^Ground admission for season 1993/94, the last before Stamford Bridge became an all-seater stadium
~ Not including discounts for Club members

— £264 PER SECOND —

Signed on a Bosman free transfer from Barcelona shortly before Gianluca Vialli's dismissal as Chelsea manager, Dutch defender Winston Bogarde endured a miserable four years at Stamford Bridge, making just four starts for the club. To make matters worse, all four games Bogarde began ended in defeat for the Blues:

Date	Result
September 17 2000	Chelsea 0 Leicester City 2
September 28 2000	St Gallen 2 Chelsea 0
November 1 2000	Liverpool 2 Chelsea 1
November 25 2000	Everton 2 Chelsea 1

Yet there were compensations – notably in the form of a salary package estimated to be in the region of £2 million per year. If this figure is correct, Bogarde was paid at a rate of £15,841 for every minute or £264 per second he appeared on the pitch for the Chelsea first team. Nice work if you can get it!

— LEAGUE CUP BOYCOTT —

In the early years of the League Cup the competition was seen by many big clubs as an unwanted addition to an already crowded fixture list. Chelsea were among those to boycott the competition, failing to enter a team in the following seasons:

1961/62
1962/63
1965/66

In the last of these three seasons Chelsea were the holders of the League Cup trophy but still decided against defending their title. This decision was taken because the club had qualified for the Fairs Cup (the precursor of the UEFA Cup) and it was felt that competing in the League Cup as well would cause difficulties with fixture congestion.

— CAPITAL BRAGGING RIGHTS —

"One team in London!" may be a favourite chant of the Chelsea faithful but, if truth be told, the Blues have rarely been the capital's top team. In fact, since the end of the Second World War Chelsea have only finished as London's highest-placed club on ten occasions:

Year	Chelsea's Position	Second-placed London club and position
1954	8th	Arsenal (12th)
1955	1st	Arsenal (9th)
1964	5th	Arsenal (8th)
1965	3rd	Tottenham (6th)
1966	5th	Tottenham (8th)
1968	6th	Tottenham (7th)
1970	3rd	Tottenham (11th)
2005	1st	Arsenal (2nd)
2006	1st	Arsenal (4th)
2007	2nd	Arsenal (4th)

— SAMPLE ADVERTS FROM THE
CHELSEA PROGRAMME —

1975/76
London Lady Escorts, 52 Shaftesbury Avenue W1
'Attractive and discreet company – for any occasion'

1980/81
The Samaritans, Putney Branch, 106 Felsham Road SW15
'Feeling desperate? Talk to the Samaritans – any time day or night'

1982/83
The Lotte Berk Studio, 465 Fulham Road SW6
'A unique system of exercises to help you achieve a super shapely body'

1993/94
Wrapped in Plastic, 218 Fulham Road SW10
'For all the latest chart releases, CDs, cassettes and videos'

2004/05
Battersea Dogs Home, 4 Battersea Park Road SW8
'By supporting Battersea Dogs Home, you can help dogs like Spot to find loving new homes'

— 1907: A FIRST PROMOTION —

In only their second year as a Football League club Chelsea gained promotion to the First Division along with champions Nottingham Forest. For the final match of the season at home to Gainsborough Trinity, the Chelsea programme celebrated this achievement, with the following words:

"There is no necessity for us to perform a solo on the Chelsea trumpet. That tune has been played with orchestral effects by the full band of the public press and our legion of followers. That the Chelsea team has accomplished a wonderful feat in gaining promotion, in the second year of the club's existence, to the Premier League is beyond cavil."

Top Six: 1906/07

	P	W	D	L	F	A	Pts
Nottingham Forest	38	28	4	6	74	36	60
Chelsea	38	26	5	7	80	34	57
Leicester City	38	20	8	10	62	39	48
West Bromwich Albion	38	21	5	12	83	45	47
Bradford City	38	21	5	12	70	53	47
Wolverhampton Wanderers	38	17	7	14	66	53	41

— CHELSEA KIT SPONSORS —

Glenn Hoddle wears the Amiga 1993/94 shirt with pride

Starting with Gulf Air during the promotion season of 1983/84, ten companies have sponsored Chelsea's shirts:

Gulf Air (second half of 1983/84 season)
Bai Lin Tea (selected matches during1986/87)
Grange Farm (selected matches during1986/87)
Simod (selected matches during1986/87)
Commodore (1987–93)
Amiga (1993/94)
Coors (1994–97)
Autoglass (1997–2001)
Emirates (2001–2005)
Samsung (2005–)

— GREAVSIE'S EIGHT-GOAL SALVO —

In season 1959/60 Jimmy Greaves notched an incredible total of eight goals in two First Division against the same team, Preston North End. The Lancashire side visited Stamford Bridge on the opening day of the campaign and came away with a point from an entertaining 4–4 draw, Greaves scoring three of the Blues' goals. In the return fixture a week before Christmas, Jimmy did even better, claiming all five of Chelsea's goals in a dramatic 5–4 win at Deepdale.

Greaves' eight-goal haul against the Lilywhites established a new Chelsea record, surpassing the seven goals George Hilsdon managed in total against Glossop North End in 1906/07.

Peter Osgood also hit eight goals in two European Cup Winners Cup matches against Luxembourg minnows Jeunesse Hautcharage in September 1971. Ossie grabbed a hat-trick in the Blues' 8–0 away leg victory and followed that up with five goals in Chelsea's record 13–0 win at the Bridge in the return.

— SEXY FAVES —

During the 2000/01 season the matchday Chelsea programme asked the players to nominate the three sexiest people in the world. The most popular nominations were:

Jennifer Lopez
Cameron Diaz
Jennifer Anniston
Kelly Brooke

The only male to be nominated was Brad Pitt (one of the three choices of Roberto di Matteo).

— SCANDAL SITES —

Over the years Chelsea stars have been involved in numerous bust ups with the management, run-ins with the police and various other assorted scandalous episodes. Some of the most infamous incidents took place at the following locations:

- **Blackpool, April 1965**: Manager Tommy Docherty sent home eight players, including Terry Venables, George Graham and John Hollins, when they disobeyed his instruction to stay in the team hotel and instead went out drinking on the Golden Mile.

- **Old Street Police Station, 1968**: Tommy Baldwin was charged with assault after throwing a vodka bottle out of a speeding car and then being involved in a scuffle with police at the station. Baldwin was sentenced to four months in prison, although following an appeal the sentence was suspended.
- **Barbarella's restaurant, Fulham Road, January 1969**: Peter Osgood, John Boyle and Charlie Cooke spent a drunken afternoon here when they should have been receiving treatment at the Bridge for minor injuries. Manager Dave Sexton was not amused and dropped the trio for the Blues' next match at Southampton – which Chelsea lost 5–0.
- **King's Road, January 1972**: Peter Osgood was arrested by the police and charged with being drunk and disorderly after singing 'We're on our way to Wembley!' following Chelsea's epic League Cup semi-final defeat of Tottenham. The case against Osgood was dismissed by the magistrate the next day.
- **Scribes West nightclub, Kensington, October 1994**: After hailing a taxi outside the club owned by then England manager Terry Venables, Dennis Wise became involved in a fracas with the driver. Wise was arrested and charged with criminal damage and assault. Initially found guilty and sentenced to three months in prison, his conviction was overturned on appeal.
- **Posthouse Hotel, Heathrow, September 2001**: Four Chelsea players – Frank Lampard, John Terry, Eidur Gudjohnsen and Jody Morris – were each fined two weeks' wages after their drunken antics in the hotel bar offended American tourists waiting for flights home following the Al-Qaida attacks on the US on September 11th.
- **The Wellington Club, Knightsbridge, January 2002**: John Terry and Jody Morris were involved in an incident with a bouncer at the club which led to them appearing at Middlesex Guildhall Crown Court in August 2002. Terry was charged with a number of offences, including wounding with intent to cause grievous bodily harm, while Morris was charged with affray. The jury found both players not guilty on all counts.
- **B & Q store, Dartford, January 2007**: While on loan at Portsmouth Blues defender Glen Johnson was spotted putting a toilet seat into a box with a lower price tag by a 74-year-old security guard. Along with Millwall striker Ben May, he also hid a set of taps under a sink to avoid paying for them. Police were called to the scene and the pair were handed on the spot fines of £80 each.

— FAN POWER —

Fans often complain that their opinions are ignored, but on a number of occasions when Chelsea supporters have made their feelings clear the powers-that-be have taken note:

- **August 1971:** Shed idol Peter Osgood was put on the transfer list by Chelsea boss Dave Sexton for "lack of effort". Fans demonstrated outside the Bridge with placards reading 'Don't go, Ossie!' and 'Sexton must relent'. Sexton did relent and took Osgood off the list.

- **May 1981:** After watching their side fail to score in the last nine matches of the season, 2,000 Chelsea fans invaded the Stamford Bridge pitch on the final day of the campaign calling for chairman Brian Mears to resign. Having initially stated that he had no intention of standing down, Mears eventually quit on 2 June 1981.

- **May 1996:** Following Glenn Hoddle's appointment as England coach, press reports suggested that former Arsenal manager George Graham was the favourite to succeed him at Stamford Bridge. The fans, though, were adamant that they didn't want the defensive-minded Graham and instead hailed star player Ruud Gullit as their preferred choice in the final home game of the season. A few days later Gullit was appointed player/manager of the Blues.

- **2003/04 season:** While media speculation linked England coach Sven Goran Eriksson with the Chelsea job, supporters made it clear that the bespectacled, bed-hopping Swede was not wanted at Stamford Bridge. Chants of 'We don't need Eriksson' rang out at several matches and the Chelsea hierarchy eventually settled on Jose Mourinho as a replacement for Claudio Ranieri.

— BLUE GOOGLIES —

Number of web site pages produced by a Google search for the following Chelsea names:

Roman Abramovich: 1.27 million
Jose Mourinho: 1.3 million
John Terry: 67.5 million
Joe Cole: 3.78 million
Kerry Dixon: 1.03 million
Ron 'Chopper' Harris: 251,000
Willie 'Fatty' Foulke: 376
Stamford the Lion: 575,000

— BLUE ROAD MAP —

Selected names appearing in the London A-Z with a Chelsea connection:

Roman Road, E2
Bates Crescent, SW16
Bridge Street, SW1
Cole Close, SE28
Parker Street, WC2
Duff Street, E14
Wise Lane, NW7
Sinclair Gardens, W14
Furlong Road, N7
Townsend Avenue, N14
Dixon Close, E6
Hudson Place, SE18

— FLIRTATION WITH DISASTER —

In season 1982/83 Chelsea only narrowly avoided relegation to the old Third Division. Eventually, thanks to a 1–0 win at Bolton and a 0–0 draw at home to Middlesbrough in their last two games, the Blues finished two places above the drop zone. Nonetheless, Chelsea's final position of 18th in the old Second Division remains the club's lowest ever league placing. At the end of a season to forget for Blues fans the bottom six of the Second Division looked like this:

	P	W	D	L	F	A	Pts
17 Charlton Athletic	42	13	9	20	63	84	48
18 Chelsea	**42**	**11**	**14**	**17**	**51**	**61**	**47**
19 Grimsby Town	42	12	11	19	45	70	47
20 Rotherham United	42	10	15	17	45	68	45
21 Burnley	42	12	8	22	56	66	44
22 Bolton Wanderers	42	11	11	20	42	61	44

— CAPITAL BRAGGING RIGHTS 2 —

Chelsea, along with Arsenal, are now firmly established as one of the two major powers in London football. Yet it's only a few short years ago that the Blues were struggling to finish above such small fry as QPR, Wimbledon and Crystal Palace, let alone challenging the Gunners for top dog status in 'the smoke':

Club	Year last finished above Chelsea
Arsenal	2004
Tottenham	1996
West Ham	1996
QPR	1995
Wimbledon	1995
Crystal Palace	1992
Charlton	1989
Millwall	1989
Fulham	1983
Orient	1963
Brentford	1939
Barnet	Never

— ALLITERATIVE CHELSEA XI —

1. Steve Sherwood (1972–75)
2. Joey Jones (1982–85)
3. Paul Parker (1997)
4. Brian Bason (1972–76)
5. William Williams (1927)
6. George Graham (1964–66)
7. Damien Duff (2003–2006)
8. Didier Deschamps (1999–2000)
9. Didier Drogba (2004–)
10. Barry Bridges (1959–66)
11. Charlie Cooke (1966–78)
Manager: Billy Birrell (1939–52)

— EDDIE'S £50 GOAL —

Midfielder Eddie Newton only scored one goal for Chelsea during the 1996/97 season, but he couldn't have chosen a bigger game in which to find the net – the 1997 FA Cup Final against Middlesbrough. Not only did the goal wrap up a 2–0 victory for the Blues, it also saved him £50 in a 'season's goals' bet with team-mate Frank Sinclair. In the event, both players finished the season on one goal each, so neither player won the money. "I was expecting to take £50 off him after the game," complained Sinclair afterwards, "and the geezer's come up and scored in the FA Cup Final. He's so stingy he had to score."

— KEN'S DOUBLE NATIONALITY —

Ken Armstrong, a key member of the Blues' 1955 championship-winning team, is the only Chelsea player to have won international caps for two countries. In 1955 Armstrong played his only game for England, in the 7–2 thrashing of Scotland at Wembley. In 1957, after setting a then Chelsea appearance record of 402 matches, he emigrated to New Zealand and, the following year, made the first of 13 international appearances for the Kiwis.

— CHELSEA DOG OWNERS —

Joe Cole: Bin, a bulldog
Hernan Crespo: Toby, a shitzu
Frank Lampard: Rocco and Daphney, French mastiffs
Claudio Ranieri: Shark
Juan Sebastian Veron: Baloo, a golden retriever
Ashley Cole: Buster, a chihuahua

— OLD TRAFFORD FINALS —

The FA Cup Final has only been played twice at Old Trafford, in 1915 and 1970, and on both occasions Chelsea appeared in the final. The 1915 final between the Blues and Sheffield United should have been played at Crystal Palace but was switched to Manchester to make attendance more difficult for London-based fans, so limiting absenteeism by workers carrying out essential war work during World War I.

In 1970 the FA Cup Final replay was played at Old Trafford after the Wembley pitch had been judged too poor to stage a second match. The problem stemmed from a misguided decision by the stadium authorities to allow the Horse of the Year Show to be held at the Twin Towers venue.

— PREMIERSHIP BOGEYMEN —

Since the Premiership began in 1992 only three opposition strikers have managed to score a hat-trick against the Blues. The dastardly trio are:

Year	Player	Result
1997	Dion Dublin	Coventry City 3 Chelsea 2
1997	Patrik Berger	Liverpool 4 Chelsea 2
1999	Kanu	Chelsea 2 Arsenal 3

— CHELSEA SIGNINGS PROMPT
TRANSFER DEADLINE —

In a desperate bid to avoid relegation Chelsea splashed out the then sizeable sum of £3,300 on three new players in April 1910. Marshall McEwan, English McConnell and Bob Whittingham all appeared in the final encounter of the season away to fellow strugglers Tottenham which Spurs won 2–1.

Although the signings had not, ultimately, altered Chelsea's fate, the Football League decided that similar panic buys would not be allowed in the future and promptly introduced the transfer deadline.

— KIT DISASTERS —

Chelsea's royal blue home kit has long been considered as one of the most stylish in the league. The Blues, though, have committed a few fashion blunders over the years and, on occasions, have even been reduced to borrowing their opponents' kit!:

- In a fifth round FA Cup replay against Chesterfield in 1950, Chelsea wore Fulham shirts complete with their neighbours' crest. This odd episode stemmed from the FA's insistence that, in the event of a kit clash, both teams should change colours. Unfortunately, the second choice kits also clashed so, following a toss of the coin, Chelsea were forced to look elsewhere and, lacking a third-choice kit, had to make do with a loan from the Cottagers.
- In the 1966 FA Cup semi-final against Sheffield Wednesday at Villa Park Chelsea wore a blue-and-black striped kit based on Inter Milan's colours. The Blues lost the match 2–0 and never wore the kit again.
- In 1973 Chelsea boss Dave Sexton introduced a striking new away kit for the Blues: red shirts, white shorts and green socks. The colours matched those worn by the Hungarian side of 1953 which famously thrashed England 6–3 at Wembley. Sadly, the Magyars' magic failed to rub off on the Blues, who won just eight away league games in the two seasons they wore the kit.
- Between 1994 and 1996 Chelsea wore an orange and grey away strip which many fans consider their worst ever. Star player Ruud Gullit, who once said he only decided to join the Blues because of their stylish white socks, must have been appalled by this fashion faux pas.

- On 9 April 1997 Chelsea were all set to play Coventry at Highfield Road when the referee decided that the Blues' first-choice blue kit clashed with the home team's sky blue outfit. Having failed to pack their second choice yellow kit, Chelsea were forced to wear Coventry's red-and-black 'chessboard' away shirts, complete with Peugeot sponsorship logo. After a 15–minute delay while the Chelsea players changed, Coventry (home) beat Coventry (away) 3–1.

— LEADING SCORERS IN ALL COMPETITIONS —

League: Bobby Tambling, 164 goals
FA Cup: Bobby Tambling, 25 goals
League Cup: Kerry Dixon, 25 goals
Premiership: Jimmy Floyd Hasselbaink, 69 goals
Europe: Peter Osgood, 16 goals

— TV NICKNAMES —

A number of Chelsea players have had nicknames derived from popular TV characters. These include:

John Hollins: Ena (after the *Coronation Street* gossip, Ena Sharples)
Eddie McCreadie: Clarence (after the squint-eyed lion in *Daktari*)
John Boyle: Trampas (a character in the 60s Western series, *The Virginian*)
Garry Stanley: Starsky (the character played by Stanley-lookalike Paul Michael Glazer in *Starsky and Hutch*)
David Lee: Rodders (after Rodney Trotter, the Nicholas Lyndhurst character in *Only Fools and Horses*)
Graeme Le Saux: Bergerac, usually shortened to 'Berge' (like Le Saux the TV detective was from the Channel Islands)

— RODDERS: THE NEW BOTHAM? —

On 4 July 1995 the then Chelsea squad branched out into another sport, taking on the Kodak Cricket Club at the summer game. Star of the show for the Blues was David 'Rodders' Lee who scored an unbeaten century and took two wickets in his only over. The match finished in a draw. For some reason, Wisden didn't see fit to include the scores in its annual round up, so here they are for the first time in print:

Chelsea

1.	Kevin Hitchcock c Harwood b Geary	16
2.	Darren Barnard c Green b Harwood	14
3.	Craig Burley c Blackeby b Patel	33
4.	Graham Stuart b Barnard	27
5.	(Guest) Spencer c Bellis b Hawkridge	59
6.	David Lee retired	129
7.	Gareth Hall run out	0
8.	Graham Rix not out	18
9.	(Guest) Phillips b Hawkridge	13
10.	Kevin Wilson b Geary	2
	Extras	14
	Total	325–8 dec

Did not bat: Richie Sexton

Fall of wickets: 1–27, 2–35, 3–78, 4–98, 5–290, 6–293, 7–320, 8–325

Kodak Cricket Club

1.	Hawkridge b Sexton	11
2.	Ward c Barnard b Wilson	7
3.	Blackeby c Hall b Spencer	41
4.	Green c Burley b Barnard	112
5.	Harwood c sexton b Rix	2
6.	Barnard c Burley b Barnard	47
7.	Bellis not out	17
8.	Geary c Spencer b Lee	15
9.	Davies b Lee	0
10.	Patel not out	7
	Extras	8
	Total	267–8

Fall of wickets: 1–4, 2–19, 3–102, 4–104, 5–209, 6–238, 7–260, 8–260

— PROGRAMME FACTS —

- The first Chelsea programme, entitled 'The Chelsea FC Chronicle', was published for a friendly match against Liverpool at Stamford Bridge on 4 September 1905. The opening words read: "They're off, Chelsea's opening home match was a friendly pipe-opener against Liverpool at Stamford Bridge. One of the linesmen was none other than J.J. Bentley Esquire, President of the Football League!"
- On 25 December 1948 for the visit of Portsmouth Chelsea became the first club to issue a 16–page magazine-style programme. It cost six old pence (2.5p).

- The ever-expanding page numbers were increased to 20 in 1975, 24 in 1978, 32 in 1985, 40 in 1990, 56 in 1994, 64 in 1997, 68 in 1999 and 74 in 2005. The larger-size page format was first introduced in 1974, although the programme reverted to a smaller, pocket-size format between 1980 and 1983.
- Editors of the programme since 1948 are: Albert Sewell (1948–80), Hugh Hastings (1980–86), Colin Benson (1986–89), Dennis Signey OBE (1989–91), Hayters news agency (1991–94), Neil Barnett (1994–2004), Andrew Winter (2004), Chris Deary (acting editor, 2004) and Lee Berry (2004–).
- In the 1972/73 season Chelsea's 26 home matches in all competitions were watched by a total of 780,934 spectators who bought 770,932 programmes. This represented an average programme sale over the season of 99%, which is believed to be a world record for any club.
- When Chelsea played away to Jeunesse Hautcharage in the European Cup Winners Cup in 1971 the Luxembourg side produced a 160–page programme, the longest ever for a Blues match.
- The manager's programme column was introduced as a regular feature at the start of the 1980/81 season when Geoff Hurst was the Blues' boss.
- The captain's column didn't appear until the 1984/85 season when Colin Pates was the skipper.

— FORTRESS STAMFORD BRIDGE —

On five occasions Chelsea have gone through a whole league season without being beaten at Stamford Bridge:

Season	P	W	D	L	F	A
1910/11	19	17	2	0	48	7
1976/77	21	15	6	0	51	22
2004/05	19	14	5	0	35	6
2005/06	19	18	1	0	47	9
2006/07	19	12	7	0	37	11

The Blues' extraordinary form at the Bridge over the last three seasons under Jose Mourinho has seen them equal Liverpool's all-time record of 63 consecutive undefeated home league games, set between 1978 and 1981. Chelsea's impressive run began after a 2–1 defeat by Arsenal on 21 February 2004, although the first match in the sequence was not played until 20 March when the Blues beat Fulham 2–1.

— SAVED BY THE WAR! —

When World War I broke out it initially had little effect on English football and the 1914/15 season was completed as normal. The campaign was a mixed one for the Blues: on a positive note, Chelsea reached the FA Cup Final for the first time, losing to Sheffield United at Old Trafford; less impressively, the Blues finished second bottom of the First Division and looked set to be relegated along with Tottenham.

However, Chelsea's future and that of all the other English league clubs, was put on hold by events across the Channel. The fighting in Flanders between the allied and German armies had continued throughout the 1914/15 season and showed no signs of abating. In the summer of 1915 the Football League decided it had no choice but to suspend league football until the hostilities ceased.

After the war the Football League was restructured, with the First Division being increased from 20 to 22 clubs. Two extra clubs were required to fill the division, and Chelsea were given a reprieve. The other fortunate club was Arsenal who, despite only having finished fifth in the Second Division in 1914/15, were promoted along with Derby and Preston. The Blues, meanwhile, made the most of their lucky escape, finishing 3rd in the first season after the war (1919/20), the highest position in the club's history at that point.

— MOONING BLUES —

• Returning to Chelsea for Eddie Niedzwiecki's testimonial game in May 1989, former fans' favourite David Speedie dropped his shorts in response to chants from the Shed. The Football Association fined him £750, although Chelsea chairman Ken Bates generously picked up the tab.

• After scoring Chelsea's opening goal away to Coventry City in August 1997 Frank Sinclair celebrated by dropping his shorts. Again, the FA took a dim view of the incident and fined Frank £750.

— AN EARLY BATH —

Over the years Chelsea players have had their moments when they haven't seen eye-to-eye with referees. Here are some Blues who later regretted getting on the wrong side of the man in the middle:

- Joey Jones was sent off in his first match for the Blues away to Carlisle on 30 October 1982.
- Much loved Chelsea idol Dennis Wise fared little better – he got his marching orders in his second match for the club after a scrap with Crystal Palace's Andy Gray at Selhurst Park on 28 August 1990.
- Centre-half John Dempsey was sent off in his first ever European match, away to Aris Salonika of Greece on 19 September 1970.
- Chelsea finished a home match against Coventry City on 14 March 1992 with just nine men. Both skipper Andy Townsend and striker Clive Allen were sent off for arguing with the match officials. Seven years later, on 16 October 1999, Chelsea were again reduced to nine men when Marcel Desailly and Dennis Wise were dismissed at Anfield.
- Talking of Wisey, the former Chelsea captain may be a Bridge legend but he had an appalling disciplinary record with the Blues. In an 11–year career with the Londoners he was sent off on no fewer than nine occasions, with a low point of four dismissals during the 1998/99 season:

Year	Result	Reason dismissed
1990	Crystal Palace 2 Chelsea 1	Violent conduct
1993	West Ham 1 Chelsea 0	Foul play
1994	Newcastle 4 Chelsea 2	Foul and abusive language
1998	Atletico Madrid 4 Chelsea 0	Foul play
1998	Chelsea 4 Aston Villa 1	Foul play
1998	Everton 0 Chelsea 0	Two yellow cards
1999	Chelsea 4 Oxford 2	Deliberate handball
1999	Liverpool 1 Chelsea 0	Dangerous play
2000	Chelsea 2 Leicester 1	Two yellow cards

— LIVES THAT WERE TOUCHED BY THE HAND OF CHELSEA —

What the stars' autobiographies said about the Blues:

"I was a Chelsea fanatic. When my turn came to choose the bedroom décor coincided with their FA Cup winning run of 1970/71 (sic), I gave Mum a Chelsea rosette so that she could buy the wallpaper and bed covers in exactly the right colours."
  Ian Botham, (Botham: My Autobiography, CollinsWillow, 1994)

"In my teens I was a Chelsea season-ticket holder. I remember sitting in the 'old' North Stand on the corner and seeing a seventeen-year-old Jimmy Greaves score four goals against Portsmouth on Christmas morning."

John Motson (Motty's Diary, Virgin Books, 1996)

"Games at Chelsea are inevitably dismal. You stand there on the huge crumbling terrace, your feet stiffening and then actually burning in the cold, with the Chelsea fans jeering and gesturing at you, and you wonder why you bothered."

Nick Hornby (Fever Pitch, Victor Gollancz, 1992)

"The disappointment was incredible. I went straight to the dressing-room and kicked open the door. I've never been more upset over losing a game."

Jack Charlton, on his reaction to losing the 1970 FA Cup Final to Chelsea (The Autobiography, Partridge Press, 1996)

"Dad supported Arsenal but I was a Chelsea fan. I'll never forget the first game I saw. It was Chelsea at home to West Ham, and I remember Clive Walker was in the side. He was a player who excited me, and I couldn't wait to go back."

Paul Merson (Rock Bottom, Bloomsbury, 1995)

"I am bored blue by the company of businessmen. I have absolutely nothing in common with them. I don't like sitting around with a glass in my hand. I don't understand references to Chelsea FC."

Alan Clark (Diaries, Weidenfeld & Nicholson, 1993)

"The area was undergoing plutocratic Italianisation (Milan being the model, not Florence or Rome), deriving its character from Chelsea Football Club – from Roberto di Matteo, from Gianfranco Zola, from Gianluca Vialli. On the street everybody is impeccably groomed, beautifully shod, wasp-waisted, leather-jacketed. They all look as though they earn thirty thousand pounds a week and eat pasta three times a day."

Matin Amis on the Fulham Road (Experience, Jonathan Cape, 2000)

— INTERNATIONALS ALL —

Chelsea first fielded a side entirely made up of internationals away to Coventry City on 15 August 1998. The Blues' team lined up as follows: De Goey (Holland); Ferrer (Spain), Desailly (France), Leboeuf (France), Le Saux (England); Poyet (Uruguay), Wise (England), Di Matteo (Italy), Babayaro (Nigeria); Vialli (Italy), Casiraghi (Italy). Both playing substitiutes, Flo (Norway) and Zola (Italy) were also internationals. Despite this impressive line-up, Chelsea still lost the match 2–1.

— GEORGE'S BARREN RUN —

In the days of baggy shorts, steel-capped boots and laced-up balls, defenders weren't expected to do anything else except defend. Right-back George W Smith, who played for the Blues in the 1920s, took this philosophy to the extreme by failing to score a single goal in 370 games for the club. No other outfield Chelsea player – yes, not even Robert Fleck or Chris Sutton – has been so unprolific in front of goal.

— CHELSEA MONOPOLY —

In 2005 Chelsea launched its own version of the popular board game Monopoly. Instead of Mayfair, Park Lane and the Old Kent Road, players can purchase former and current Blues and different parts of Stamford Bridge. Sample prices, which tend towards the low side, include:

Petr Cech £60
John Terry £160
Dennis Wise £200
Matthew Harding Stand £200
Kerry Dixon £260
Peter Osgood £300
Gianfranco Zola £350
Jose Mourinho £400

— FOOTBALLERS' DAUGHTERS CALLED 'CHELSEA' —

Beatrice Chelsea Petrescu, daughter of Dan (Chelsea 1995–2000)
Chelsea Smethurst, daughter of Derek (Chelsea 1970–71)
Chelsea Johnston, daughter of Craig (ex-Liverpool)
Chelsea Merson, daughter of Paul (ex-Arsenal)

— HILLY'S DOUBLE HAT-TRICK —

Chelsea's first goalscoring superstar, striker George 'Gatling Gun' Hilsdon, remains the only player in the club's history to have hit a double hat-trick. George's 'super six' came in the Blues' 9–1 demolition of Midland League side Worksop in the FA Cup first round on 11 January 1908. Five players, including Hilsdon, have scored five goals in a match for Chelsea and they are . . .

Year	Player	Result
1906	George Hilsdon	Chelsea 9 Glossop 2
1958	Jimmy Greaves	Chelsea 6 Wolves 2
1959	Jimmy Greaves	Preston 4 Chelsea 5
1961	Jimmy Greaves	Chelsea 7 WBA 1
1966	Bobby Tambling	Aston Villa 2 Chelsea 6
1971	Peter Osgood	Chelsea 13 Jeunesse Hautcharage 0
1989	Gordon Durie	Walsall 0 Chelsea 7

— TATTOO BLUE —

Chelsea players whose bodies are adorned by tattoos include:

Joey Jones: Somewhat at variance with his tough guy image, the hard-tackling defender always wore a long sleeved shirt during his spell at Chelsea in the early 1980s. The reason? Hidden by his blue shirt was a tattoo of a liver bird on his arm, a reminder of Jones' European Cup-winning days at Liverpool.

Vinnie Jones: At the last count the footballer turned actor had five separate tattoos: a red rose on his left forearm; an image of the FA Cup marking his win with Wimbledon in 1988; a Leeds club crest commemorating his Second Division title success with the Yorkshire outfit in 1990; a Welsh dragon and feathers on his chest; and, finally, one listing the names of his immediate family in the middle of his shoulders.

Mateja Kezman: He sported an image of Christ on his right arm, but if the Serbian striker prayed for divine intervention to help him find the net at Chelsea, the Almighty clearly wasn't listening.

Juan Sebastian Veron: The onetime Argentina captain has a tattoo of radical revolutionary and fellow countryman Che Guevara on his right arm. Right on!

Gianluca Vialli: He reached the heights with the Blues, just like the soaring eagle tattoo that is perched on his right shoulder.

— CHELSEA COMEDY NAMES XI —

1. Les Fridge (1986)
2. William Dickie (1919–21)
3. Joseph Spottiswood (1920)
4. Jimmy Argue (1933–46)
5. Peter Proudfoot (1906–07)
6. Wilfred Chitty (1932–38)
7. Peter Feely (1971–72)
8. Alan Dicks (1952–57)
9. Jack Cock (1919–22)
10. Mike Brolly (1973–74)
11. Charles Dyke (1948–51)
Manager: Dave Sexton (1967–74)

— GLOOM AND DOOM —

Chelsea have been relegated from the top flight on six occasions. The matches which confirmed the Blues' drop into the old Second Division are listed below:

Year	Result	Matches Left	Final Position	Also relegated
1910	Tottenham 2 Chelsea 1	-	19th	Bolton
1924	Chelsea 3 Man City 1	-	21st	Middlesbrough
1962	Chelsea 2 Ipswich 2	2	22nd	Cardiff City
1975	Chelsea 1 Everton 1	-	21st	Carlisle, Luton
1979	Arsenal 5 Chelsea 2	5	22nd	Birmingham, QPR
1988	Chelsea 1 Middlesbrough 0*	-	18th	Portsmouth, Oxford United, Watford

* Play-off final (aggregate score, Chelsea 1 Middlesbrough 2)

— LONG TIME, NO SEE! —

After playing for Chelsea for three years between 1989 and 1992 following his £100,000 transfer from Feyenoord, Dutch centre-half Ken Monkou moved on to Southampton. Ten years later, at the age of 37, Ken returned to Stamford Bridge for a few months and, although he didn't figure in the first-team squad, made his second debut for the Blues for the reserves in a 3–1 win over Charlton in April 2002.

— HONOURS LIST —

The following Chelsea men have been awarded military or civilian honours:

Jack Cock MM (Military Medal, World War I)
Colin Hampton MM (Military Medal, World War I)
Tom Logan MM (Military Medal, World War I)
Harry Wilding MM (Military Medal, World War I)
Arthur Wileman MM (Military Medal, World War I)
Tommy Walker OBE (1960)
Geoff Hurst MBE (1979), Knighted (1998)
Ron Greenwood CBE (1981)
John Hollins MBE (1982)
Ray Wilkins MBE (1993)
Len Casey MBE (1994)
Mark Hughes MBE (1998), OBE (2004)
Dario Gradi MBE (1998)
Alan Birchenall MBE (2002)
Paul Elliott MBE (2003)
Gianfranco Zola OBE (Honorary, 2004)
Dave Sexton OBE (2005)

— A PAIR OF KINGS AT THE BRIDGE —

On 21 February 1920 King George V attended the third round FA Cup tie between Chelsea and Leicester City at the Bridge. After meeting the teams and war veterans before the match, His Majesty settled down to watch the Blues beat the Foxes 3–0.

Two weeks later Chelsea again hosted Royalty when the King of Spain, Alfonso XIII, attended the quarter-final FA Cup tie between the Blues and Bradford Park Avenue. Chelsea won the game 4–1 in front of a crowd of 61,223.

— FIRST INTERNATIONAL —

The first player to be capped for his country while playing for Chelsea was left-winger Johnny Kirwan. A member of the very first Blues team, Kirwan won four caps for Northern Ireland in 1906, making his debut in a 5-0 defeat against England in Belfast.

Among the other home countries, Chelsea's first internationals were: George Hilsdon (England, 1907), Jack Cameron (Scotland, 1909), Evan Jones (Wales, 1910) and Dick Whittaker (Republic of Ireland, 1959)

— EURO FINAL AT THE BRIDGE —

On 5 March 1958 Stamford Bridge hosted the first ever final of the Fairs Cup (later to become the UEFA Cup). The match, which was the first of two legs, was between a London Select XI and Barcelona and finished in a 2–2 draw. Three Chelsea players, Jimmy Greaves, Peter Sillett and Bobby Smith, played for the Londoners, with Greaves scoring one of the goals for the home team. Barcelona won the return 6–0 in the Nou Camp to take the trophy.

— LOCAL TALENT —

The West Stand at Stamford Bridge has six suites which are used for a variety of functions during the week and for corporate entertainment on matchdays. The suites were originally named after famous local residents, but in 2005 were re-named after legendary Chelsea players or, in Ted Drake's case, a onetime manager of the club:

Current name	Formerly named after
The Bonetti Suite	William Wilberforce, anti-slave trade campaigner (1759–1833)
The Clarke Suite	Augustus John, painter (1878–1961)
The Drake Suite	Hilaire Belloc, writer and poet (1870–1953)
The Harris Suite	Charles Kingsley, writer (1819–75)
The Hollins Suite	Captain Scott, Antarctic explorer (1868–1912)
The Tambling Suite	Sylvia Pankhurst, suffragette (1882–1960)

— THE NUMBERS GAME —

Chelsea, along with Arsenal, were the first English club to wear numbered shirts, adopting an idea developed by Gunners boss Herbert Chapman for a home game against Swansea Town on 25 August 1928. The innovation seemed to suit the Blues, who smashed four goals past Swans keeper Alex Ferguson (no relation to the cantankerous Manchester United manager) while keeping a clean sheet at the other end.

The football authorities were opposed to the innovation, however, and the experiment was not repeated until 1933 when numbered shirts were used for the FA Cup Final between Everton and Manchester City. Eventually, in 1939, the Football League made shirt numbers obligatory.

— CELERY FACT FILE —

A Chelsea tradition has developed for supporters to bring bunches of celery to cup finals the Blues are involved in – a reference, of course, to the famous 'Celery song' whose lyrics, sadly, are a little too risqué to be printed here. Instead, here are some little known facts about the Blues' vegetable of choice:

- Celery (latin name Apium Graveolens) is believed to be the same plant as *selinon*, which is mentioned in Homer's *Odyssey* around 850 BC. The English word 'celery' comes from the French 'celeri' which is itself derived from the original ancient Greek.
- The oldest record of the word 'celeri' is in a ninth century poem written in either Italy or France. The first record of celery being used as a food dates back to seventeenth century France.
- Originating in the Mediterranean, celery has been grown as a food crop for thousands of years. However, it is more difficult to grow than other vegetables, requiring a longer growing season, lots of water and preferring cooler temperatures. Without proper care, celery stalks can be very dry and stringy.
- Celery is an ideal snack for anyone trying to lose weight because the process of eating it actually consumes more calories than the vegetable itself possesses.
- A number of Chelsea fans have been arrested for throwing celery on the pitch under Section 2 of the Football (Offences) Act 1991. The act states that is an offence "to throw anything at or towards the playing area or any area in which spectators or other persons are or may be."

*A·lump
of celery*

— SIGNED FROM SCOTLAND XI —

Until the game north of the border fell into the doldrums, Chelsea had a long history of signing players from Scottish clubs. Here's a sample team:

1. Bill Robertson (signed from Arthurlie, 1946)
2. Steve Clarke (St Mirren, 1987)
3. Andy Dow (Dundee, 1993)
4. Joe McLaughlin (Morton, 1983)
5. Paul Elliott (Celtic, 1991)
6. Doug Rougvie (Aberdeen, 1984)
7. Pat Nevin (Clyde, 1983)
8. Eamonn Bannon (Hearts, 1979)
9. John Spencer (Rangers, 1992)
10. Gordon Durie (Hibernian, 1986)
11. Charlie Cooke (Dundee, 1966)

Manager: Eddie McCreadie (East Stirling, 1962)

— CHELSEA'S FIRST MATCH —

Chelsea played their first ever match away to Stockport County in the Second Division on 2 September 1905. By all accounts, the Edgeley Park pitch was in poor condition, with one reporter describing it as "an almost unbroken expanse of ripe plantation weed in full seed."

After a goalless first half, Stockport were given the chance to take the lead when the referee awarded a penalty kick for a foul on one of their forwards. However, Willie Foulke, Chelsea's giant goalkeeper and captain, saved the kick and then threw the ball out to a team-mate. Perhaps, he should have kicked it, as the following contemporary report describes what happened next:

"It pitched on to one of the numerous lumps and deviated sharply to the right. Foulke took the only course open to him and charged from his goal, but Stockport inside-forward, George Dodd, reached the ball first banging it straight at Robert McEwan, who would have cleared it easily but for the fact that Tommy Miller was knocked into him by a County forward at the same time, and as a result the ball glanced off McEwan's chest into the net."

Despite the suggestion of a foul, the goal was given and credited to Dodd. It remained the only goal of the game – and Chelsea's first match ended in defeat.

— TOP CAPS —

The ten players to have won the most international caps while with the Blues are:

Player	Country	Caps won with Chelsea
1. Marcel Desailly	France	74
2. Frank Lampard	England	52
3. William Gallas	France	48
4. Dan Petrescu	Romania	44
5. Tore Andre Flo	Norway	38
6. John Terry	England	37
7. Eidur Gudjohnsen	Iceland	36
8. Jesper Gronkjaer	Denmark	35
9. Frank Leboeuf	France	32
10. Mikael Forssell	Finland	31

— CHELSEA OLD BOYS —

Currently managed by 1980s defender Gary Chivers, Chelsea Old Boys play charity matches throughout the year at grounds in the London area and beyond. The side is largely made up of evergreen players from the seventies and eighties, including Ray Wilkins, Garry Stanley and Clive Walker, although younger players such as David Lee, Jason Cundy and Gareth Hall have recently emerged from the club's 'youth academy'.

In 2004 the Old Boys enjoyed their greatest success to date when they won the Build Center Masters Cup in Sheffield, beating Wolves 2–1 in the final thanks to two goals by Kevin Wilson.

The club has its own website (*www.chelseaoldboys.co.uk*) where fans can sign up as 'pay to play' players – £150 gets you a run out with your old heroes and a Chelsea shirt signed by all the team.

— LEAGUE OF NATIONS —

Internationals from the following 42 countries have been on Chelsea's books: All Ireland, Argentina, Australia, Austria, Cameroon, CIS, Croatia, Czech Republic, Denmark, England, Finland, France, Germany, Georgia, Ghana, Holland, Iceland, Israel, Italy, Ivory Coast, Jamaica, Liberia, Morocco, New Zealand, Nigeria, Northern Ireland, Norway, Phillipines, Portugal, Republic of Ireland, Russia, Scotland, Serbia and Montenegro, South Africa, Spain, Sweden, Switzerland, Turkey, Ukraine, Uruguay, USA and Wales.

— COUNT THE CROWD —

Chelsea's Second Division match with Orient on 5 May 1982 was attended by just 6,009 fans, the lowest gate for a league game at the Bridge since the war. Other all-time attendance lows include:

Year	Competition	Result	Crowd att
1905	FA Cup	Chelsea 6 Ist Battalion Grenadiers 1	5,000
1906	Football League	Chelsea 4 Lincoln 2	3,000
1960	League Cup	Chelsea 4 Workington 2	5,630
1991	Full Members Cup	Chelsea 1 Luton 1	3,849
1994	Premiership	Chelsea 1 Coventry 2	8,923

— CHELSEA'S FIRST EVER LINE UP, V STOCKPORT COUNTY (AWAY), 2 SEPTEMBER 1905 —

Goalkeeper: Willie Foulke (captain)
Right-back: Robert Mackie
Left-back: Robert McEwan
Right-half: George Key
Centre-half: Bob McRoberts
Left-half: Tommy Miller
Outside-right: Martin Moran
Inside-right: John Tait Robertson
Centre-forward: David Copeland
Inside-left: Jimmy Windridge
Outside-left: John Kirwan

— OTHER SPORTS STAGED AT STAMFORD BRIDGE —

American Football
Athletics
Baseball
Cricket
Cycling
Greyhound racing
Midget car racing
Rugby league
Rugby union
Speedway

— ON THE BRINK —

Chelsea have had a few narrow escapes from relegation but none as tight as the one the Blues pulled off in 1951. With four games to go the Londoners were stuck at the bottom of the First Division, four points behind Sheffield Wednesday (21st) and six behind Everton (20th). The trap door to the Second Division was beckoning.

Remarkably, though, the Blues managed to win their next three fixtures at home to Liverpool (1–0) and Wolves (2–1) and away to Fulham (2–1) to move level on points with Wednesday and to within two points of Everton. On the final day of the season Chelsea beat Bolton 4–0 at the Bridge, while Everton, who only needed a draw to survive, were thrashed 6–0 at Hillsborough. With all three teams level on 32 points, goal average was required to separate the teams and Chelsea narrowly came out on top:

First Division bottom three 1950/51

	P	W	D	L	F	A	Pts	Goal Ave
20 Chelsea	42	12	8	22	53	65	32	0.815
21 Sheffield Weds	42	12	8	22	64	83	32	0.771
22 Everton	42	12	8	22	48	86	32	0.558

— LEFT-FOOTED CHELSEA XI —

1. Petr Cech (2004–)
2. Celestine Babayaro (1997–2004)
3. Wayne Bridge (2003–)
4. Andy Townsend (1990–93)
5. Colin Pates (1979–87)
6. Mickey Droy (1971–85)
7. Graeme Le Saux (1989–2003)
8. Alan Birchenall (1967–70)
9. Bobby Tambling (1959–70)
10. Mike Fillery (1979–83)
11. Peter Houseman (1963–75)
Manager: Eddie McCreadie (1975–77)

— CAN WE PLAY YOU EVERY DAY? —

In 1964 Tommy Docherty's Chelsea side went on a post-season tour of the Caribbean, playing a series of fairly undemanding games against local opposition as well as a number of games against fellow tourists Wolves. In fact, the two English teams must have been sick of the sight of each other as they met no fewer than five times in the space of two weeks. The results of these games, and the exotic venues, are given below:

Date	Result	Venue
23 May	Chelsea 1 Wolves 3	Barbados
27 May	Chelsea 3 Wolves 2	Trinidad
29 May	Chelsea 2 Wolves 4	Jamaica
2 June	Chelsea 3 Wolves 0	Jamaica
6 June	Chelsea 2 Wolves 0	Haiti

— DEATH OR GLORY —

Chelsea's penalty shoot-out results in major competitions:

Year	Competition	Result	Shoot-out score
1983	Milk Cup	Chelsea 2	Chelsea 6
		Leicester 2 (agg)	Leicester 5
1985	Full Members Cup	WBA 2	WBA 4
		Chelsea 2	Chelsea 5
1991	Full Members Cup	Chelsea 1	Chelsea 1
		Luton 1	Luton 4
1991	Full Members Cup	Chelsea 2	Chelsea 4
		Ipswich 2	Ipswich 3
1995	FA Cup	Chelsea 1	Chelsea 4
		Millwall 1	Millwall 5
1996	FA Cup	Newcastle 2	Newcastle 2
		Chelsea 2	Chelsea 4
1997	Charity Shield	Chelsea 1	Chelsea 2
		Man United 1	Man United 4
1997	Coca-Cola Cup	Chelsea 1	Chelsea 4
		Blackburn 1	Blackburn 1
1998	Coca-Cola Cup	Ipswich 2	Ipswich 1
		Chelsea 2	Chelsea 4
2005	Carling Cup	Chelsea 1	Chelsea 4
		Charlton 1	Charlton 5
2007	Champions League	Liverpool 1	Liverpool 4
		Chelsea 1 (agg)	Chelsea 1

— TOURING SOUTH AMERICA —

In 1929 Chelsea became one of the first British clubs to visit South America, spending six weeks in Argentina, Brazil and Uruguay. Results were mixed and so, too, were the reviews Chelsea received. After one bruising encounter in Brazil, the Blues were criticised for "displaying inferior technique, in a sporting and social sense". However, a newspaper reporter in Buenos Aires stressed that "Chelsea's record in Argentina was one of keen, honest play, and that any differences of opinion has arisen as the result purely and simply of divergence in the interpretation of the rules that govern the British game of soccer."

What is clear is that the tour helped boost morale at the club and it may not be a coincidence that in the season following the exotic trip Chelsea were promoted to the First Division after six years' absence.

— CITY OF GOALS —

Chelsea players have scored more hat-tricks against Manchester City than any other club. In total, Blues strikers have notched six trebles against the Mancunians:

Year	Player	Goals	Result
1933	Hughie Gallacher	3	Man City 1 Chelsea 4
1935	Joe Bambrick	4	Chelsea 4 Man City 2
1937	George Mills	3	Chelsea 4 Man City 4
1960	Jimmy Greaves	3	Chelsea 6 Man City 3
1984	Kerry Dixon	3	Chelsea 4 Man City 1 (Lge Cup)
1986	David Speedie	3	Chelsea 5 Man City 4 (FM Cup)

— PRESENT AND CORRECT —

Blues legends Ron Harris and John Hollins both played all Chelsea's league games in four different seasons, a club record. Chopper didn't miss a game in 1964/65, 1966/67, 1972/73 and 1974/75, while Holly was an ever-present in 1969/70, 1971/72, 1972/73 and 1973/74.

— DEADLY ENCOUNTER —

On 1 February 1936 Chelsea drew 3–3 against Sunderland at Roker Park. A few days after the game Sunderland's young goalkeeper James Thorpe died. The coroner's verdict read "death from diabetes, the death being accelerated by rough usage during the match".

— BAD DAY AT THE BRIDGE —

Over the years Chelsea supporters have endured some grim afternoons at the Bridge, none more so than when Notts County thrashed the Blues 6–0 on their home patch on 9 February 1924 – the club's biggest home defeat. Unsurprisingly, perhaps, Chelsea ended that particular season by being relegated to the Second Division.

The Blues' worst home defeat in cup competitions was a 4–0 thrashing by Birmingham City in the FA Cup on 14 February 1953 – now that's what you call a Saint Valentine's day massacre.

— ONE-CAP WONDERS —

The following Chelsea players won just a single cap for their respective countries:

Jurgen Macho* (Austria, 2002)
Ken Armstrong (England, 1955)
William Brown* (England,1924)
Jackie Crawford (England, 1931)
Willie Foulke* (England, 1897)
Harold Halse* (England, 1909)
John Hollins (England, 1967)
Percy Humphreys* (England, 1903)
Tommy Meehan (England, 1924)
Joe Payne* (England, 1937)
Seth Plum* (England, 1923)
Ken Shellito (England, 1963)
Alex Stepney* (England, 1968)
Chris Sutton* (England, 1997)
Cecil Allen* (Northern Ireland, 1935)
John Browning* (Scotland, 1914)
Peter Buchanan (Scotland, 1938)
Warren Cummings (Scotland, 2002)
Angus Douglas (Scotland, 1911)
George Henderson* (Scotland, 1904)
George Key* (Scotland, 1902)
Tom Logan* (Scotland, 1913)
Doug Rougvie* (Scotland, 1984)
Dick Whittaker ((Rep. Ireland, 1959)
Roger Freestone* (Wales, 2000)

* Cap won with a club other than Chelsea

— NUMBER 12: TWO FIRSTS —

Substitutes weren't introduced to the English game until the start of the 1965/66 season and, three games into that campaign, John Boyle became the first ever Chelsea sub to come off the bench when he replaced George Graham in the Blues' 3–0 defeat of Fulham at Craven Cottage.

The following season, winger Peter Houseman became the first Chelsea substitute to score when he netted against Charlton Athletic in a League Cup tie at Stamford Bridge on 14 September 1966. The Blues won the game 5–2.

— FACIAL FUZZ CHELSEA XI —

Hair we go: David Webb, Charlie Cooke, Alan Hudson

1. **Ed de Goey** (70s porn star-style 'tache)
2. **David Webb** (full on bushy beard)
3. **Eddie McCreadie** (Zapata moustache)
4. **Alan Hudson** (luxuriant sideburns, occasional beard)
5. **Mickey Droy** (Desperate Dan stubble)
6. **Marcel Desailly** (whispy chin tufts)
7. **Clive Walker** (strange blonde-hair-and-dark-beard combo)
8. **Kevin Wilson** (sergeant major 'tache)
9. **Mateja Kezman** ('Amish'-style beard but no moustache)
10. **Gianluca Vialli** (classic 90s goatee)
11. **Charlie Cooke** (extravagantly tapered moustache)
Manager: Jose Mourinho (too-busy-to-shave two days' stubble)

— SHOW US YOUR MEDALS —

No Chelsea player has won more medals than John Terry. To date, the popular defender has collected seven winners' medals during his time at the Bridge, his haul being made up of two FA Cups (one as a non-playing substitute in 2000), two Premierships, two Carling Cups and a Community Shield. For good measure, Terry has also picked up runners-up medals in the FA Cup and Community Shield. Let's hope he's got a decent safe . . .

— THE GOAL THAT WASN'T —

On 26 September 1970 Chelsea played Ipswich Town in a First Division game at Stamford Bridge. The Blues won the game 2–1, but one of their goals sparked a huge controversy when *Match of the Day* cameras clearly showed that Alan Hudson's shot had rebounded from the stanchion outside, rather than inside, the goal. Ipswich manager Bobby Robson was incensed, and vainly pleaded for the match to be replayed.

Hudson later revealed that he knew the ball had not gone in, but had decided not to inform the referee. "I'd had a couple disallowed, so I thought I deserved a bit of luck," he argued.

— DYNAMIC ATTRACTION —

On 13 November 1945 Chelsea played Moscow Dynamo in a friendly match which, despite being played on a Tuesday afternoon, attracted an enormous crowd to Stamford Bridge. An incredible 74,496 paying customers passed through the turnstiles, but many thousands more entered the ground without paying, clambering over gates and walls to get in, and then swarming onto the greyhound track surrounding the pitch to get a close-up view of the clash between representatives of the wartime allies against Nazi Germany. Other fans burst into houses overlooking the ground, desperate to get even the slightest of glimpses of the game, which finished in an exciting 3–3 draw.

Chelsea striker Tommy Lawton later described the chaotic scenes outside the ground: "When I arrived at Stamford Bridge it seemed as if everybody in London had taken the afternoon off to see the Russians. A huge surging mob were storming the gates and mounted police moved slowly among them trying to restore some semblance of order."

Unofficial estimates put the size of the crowd at around 100,000, easily surpassing Chelsea's official record crowd of 82,905 for a First Division match. Meanwhile, the full list of attendance records at Stamford Bridge is:

Competition	Year	Attendance	Result
Football League	1935	82,905	Chelsea 1 Arsenal 1
FA Cup	1911	77,952	Chelsea 3 Swindon 1
League Cup	1971	43,330	Chelsea 3 Tottenham 2
Full Members Cup	1990	15,061	Chelsea 2 Crystal Palace 0
Premiership	2004	42,328	Chelsea 4 Newcastle 0
Europe	1966	59,541	Chelsea 2 AC Milan 1

— PRINCESS MARGARET – A SECRET BLUE? —

Before the 1970 FA Cup final between Chelsea and Leeds at Wembley, the Royal guest of honour, the late Princess Margaret was introduced to Blues skipper Ron Harris. "While we were chatting she said she hoped Chelsea would win," Ron said later.

As it turned out, Princess Margaret couldn't have been much of a Chelsea fan as she didn't bother attending the replay at Old Trafford, leaving the cup to be presented to Chopper by the President of the Football Association. On the four occasions Chelsea have won the cup the trophy has been presented by:

FA Cup-winning year	Chelsea captain	Cup presented by
1970	Ron Harris	Dr Andrew Stephen
1997	Dennis Wise	HRH Duke of Kent
2000	Dennis Wise*	HRH Duke of Kent
2007	John Terry	Prince William

* In 2000, Wise was assisted in collecting the cup by his son, Henry

— VIP VISITORS —

Numerous distinguished and famous people have attended matches at Stamford Bridge, including:

1920   King George V
1920   King Alfonso XIII of Spain
1972   Harold Wilson, former Prime Minister, Great Britain
1972   Raquel Welch, Hollywood film star
1976   Dr Henry Kissinger, American Secretary of State
1984   Boy George, singer
1991   John Major, Prime Minister, Great Britain
1995   Tony Blair, then Leader of the Opposition
2003   Sir Clive Woodward, England rugby manager
2006   Pele, Brazilian football legend
2007   President Kufour of Ghana
2007   Prince Harry

— A MINUTE'S SILENCE —

Among the individuals and groups to have been remembered with a minute's silence before kick-off at Stamford Bridge are:

	Date	Match
Hillsborough disaster victims	22 April 1989	Chelsea 1 Leeds 0
Sir Matt Busby	22 January 1994	Chelsea 1 Aston Villa 1
Matthew Harding and friends	26 October 1996	Chelsea 3 Tottenham 1
Billy Bremner	13 December 1997	Chelsea 0 Leeds 0
Peter Sillett	19 March 1998	Chelsea 3 Betis 1
10th anniversary Hillsborough disaster	18 April 1999	Chelsea 2 Leicester 2
David Rocastle	31 March 2001	Chelsea 2 Middlesbro' 1
Mike North (referee)	21 April 2001	Chelsea 0 Charlton 1
September 11th victims	20 September 2001	Chelsea 3 Levski Sofia 0
Holly Wells and Jessica Chapman	23 August 2002	Chelsea 2 Man Utd 2
Ian Hutchinson	19 September 2002	Chelsea 2 Viking 1

	Date	Match
Beslan school victims	19 September 2004	Chelsea 0
		Tottenham 0
Tsunami victims	4 January 2005	Chelsea 2
		Middlesbro' 0
Pope John Paul II	6 April 2005	Chelsea 4
		B. Munich 2
Peter Osgood*	11 March 2006	Chelsea 2
		Tottenham 1
Alan Ball*	28 April 2007	Chelsea 2
		Bolton 2

*Minute's appreciation

— THE MEN IN BLACK —

After awarding Manchester United two penalties in the 1994 FA Cup Final, David Elleray was guaranteed a hostile reception whenever he returned to Stamford Bridge. Chelsea fans, though, have more reason to remember 1970 Cup Final referee Eric Jennings with fondness – in a physical, at times, brutal match he kept all the players on the pitch and thus played a small part in the Blues' first ever FA Cup success.

Curiously, Herbert Bamlett, the referee at the Blues' first FA Cup Final, went on to become a football manager, taking charge of Manchester United between 1927 and 1931.

FA Cup Final	Referee
1915 v Sheffield United	Herbert Bamlett (Gateshead)
1967 v Tottenham	Ken Dagnall (Bolton)
1970 v Leeds	Eric Jennings (Stourbridge)
1994 v Manchester United	David Elleray (Harrow)
1997 v Middlesbrough	Steve Lodge (Barnsley)
2000 v Aston Villa	Graham Poll (Tring)
2002 v Arsenal	Mike Riley (Leeds)
2007 v Manchester United	Steve Bennett (Orpington)

— OSSIE AND DROGS HEAD FINAL SCORERS —

Blues strikers Peter Osgood and Didier Drogba have scored more goals in cup finals than any other Chelsea player. The pair have both scored four goals in finals, Drogba equalling Ossie's long established record when he scored the winner in the 2007 FA Cup final against Manchester United at the new Wembley.

The other Chelsea players to score more than one goal in major finals are Roberto di Matteo (three goals) and Bobby Tambling (two goals).

— SUCCESSFUL START —

No Chelsea manger is ever likely to match Gianluca Vialli's record of winning a trophy in only his ninth game in charge of the Blues, the 1998 Coca-Cola Cup final against Middlesbrough at Wembley. For good measure the Italian won more silverware in just his twentieth match as Blues boss, the 1998 European Cup Winners Cup final against Stuttgart.

Somewhat less successful than Vialli was the Blues' longest-serving manager David Calderehead who was in charge of the team for 966 matches between 1907 and 1933 and won precisely nothing.

— HOT TICKET —

Seasons in which Chelsea have had the highest average home league attendance among all Football League clubs:

Season	Average attendance at Stamford Bridge
1907/8	32,894
1909/10	30,210
1911/12	27,197
1912/13	35,368
1913/14	36,131
1919/20	41,142
1921/22	39,095
1923/24	32,000
1925/26	34,190
1954/55	48,302

Remarkably, Chelsea were in the Second Division during two of these seasons (1911/12 and 1925/26), while on two other occasions (1909/10 and 1923/24) the crowds still flocked to the Bridge despite these being relegation campaigns. The average attendance during Chelsea's first championship year, 48,302, is the club's highest ever and will not be beaten unless the ground is radically redeveloped.

— THE CAT'S WHISKERS —

During his 19–year Chelsea career (1960–79) the Blues' legendary goalkeeper Peter Bonetti played 729 games for the club, keeping 208 clean sheets. His enduring quality and unfailing consistency helped him see off no fewer than 13 rivals, all of whom played at least one game for Chelsea during Bonetti's undisputed reign as 'Number One':

Goalkeeper	Matches played as Bonetti's understudy	Clean sheets
Reg Matthews+ (1956–61)	8	0
Errol McNally (1961–63)	9	0
John Dunn (1962–66)	16	3
Jim Barron (1965–66)	1	0
Mike Pinner (1961–62)	1	0
Kingsley Whiffen (1966–67)	1	0
Alex Stepney (1966)	1	1
Tommy Hughes (1965–71)	11	1
John Phillips (1970–79)	149	30
David Webb~ (1968–74)	1	1
Steve Sherwood (1971–76)	17	3
Bob Iles* (1978–83)	7	1
Petar Borota* (1979–81)	12	1

+ Also played for Chelsea before Bonetti's debut
* Also played for Chelsea after Bonetti's retirement
~ Normally outfield player

— ONE FOR THE LADIES —

In the summer of 1984 Blues striker Kerry Dixon was voted runner-up in a poll to find Britain's 'dishiest' footballer by the female readers of 'Match' magazine.

"His blond hair and lovely brown eyes are enough to send a shiver down my spine," wrote Claire Britton of York, while Katrina Stock of Twickenham reckoned, "He is the nearest thing to a perfect man I have ever seen." But not, it would seem, quite as perfect a specimen of masculinity as the poodle-permed captain of England and Manchester United, Bryan Robson, whose chiselled good looks pushed Kerry into second place.

— EIDUR'S BENCH RECORD —

Former Chelsea striker Eidur Gudjohnsen has played more games for the club as a sub (86) than any other player. Gudjohnsen passed Tore Andre Flo's previous record of 69 substitute appearances when he came on at half-time in the Blues' FA Cup fifth round tie at Newcastle on 20 February 2005.

— CUP DEFEAT, BUT BLUES STILL PROGRESS —

Strange as it may seem, the Blues once went through to the next round of the FA Cup after losing their previous game. How come? Well, in season 1945/46 FA Cup ties were played over two legs and after beating West Ham 2–0 at the Bridge, Chelsea lost 1–0 at Upton Park in the second leg but still went into the draw for the fifth round.

— OFFSIDE! . . . OR, ER, MAYBE NOT —

On 31 January 1925 Chelsea played an experimental game against Arsenal at Highbury to test out various possible changes to the offside law. In the second half, the number of defending players required to keep an attacking player onside was reduced from three to two, and this change was brought into the laws of the game for the following season.

It appears that the Blues' participation in the Highbury experiment worked to their advantage at the start of the 1925/26 season as they won their first three games, wracking up an impressive goals tally of 13 for and one against in the process.

— SCOUSERS DOUBLED BY HARRY AND JOE —

Chelsea have only ever achieved three league 'doubles' over Liverpool, and in two of those seasons the Blues had the same player to thank. In 1919, Harold Brittan scored the only goal of the match on consecutive weekends to give Chelsea the points against the Reds. Then, in the 2004/05 season, Joe Cole twice came off the bench to net in the Blues' 1–0 wins at the Bridge and up at Anfield.

— BACK-TO BACK FIXTURES —

Players and managers today often complain about fixture congestion, but in the past it was common for teams to play each other on consecutive days over holiday periods. The last time the Blues played two days running was in March 1986, when they won 1–0 at Southampton on the Saturday thanks to a Colin Pates goal, and then beat Manchester City 5–4 in the Full Members Cup Final at Wembley on the Sunday. Meanwhile, selected head-to-head holiday results include:

Year	Christmas Day	Boxing Day
1912	Chelsea 1	Manchester United 4
	Manchester United 4	Chelsea 2
1923	Nottingham Forest 2	Chelsea 1
	Chelsea 0	Nottingham Forest 1
1931	Blackpool 2	Chelsea 4
	Chelsea 4	Blackpool 1
1946	Chelsea 1	Preston North End 1
	Preston North End 2	Chelsea 1
1957	Chelsea 7	Portsmouth 3
	Portsmouth 4	Chelsea 0

— BRAINS OF BRITAIN —

In season 1985/86 the Chelsea programme asked the players which specialist subject they would answer questions on if they appeared on the popular TV programme 'Mastermind'. Here are some of their replies . . .

Eddie Niedzwiecki - Greek mythology
Kevin McAllister - Battle of Bannockburn
Colin Pates - The Vietnam War
Paul Canoville - Soul Music
Doug Rougvie - EastEnders
Steve Francis - Pass

— BLING BLING BLUES —

Chelsea players to wear an ear-ring or ear-stud include:

Hernan Crespo
Michael Duberry
William Gallas
Eidur Gudjohnsen
Jimmy Floyd Hasselbaink
Glen Johnson
Mario Melchiot
Adrian Mutu
Eddie Newton
Frank Sinclair
Juan Sebastian Veron

— FIRST – AND LAST! —

The only time Chelsea have played the same club on the opening day of the season and on the last day of the league term was in 1969/70. On 9 August 1969 the Blues kicked off their campaign at Anfield, losing 4–1 to Liverpool. Eight months later, on 18 April 1970, the two sides met again at Stamford Bridge, Chelsea winning 2–1.

— FEMALE CELEBRITIES LINKED WITH CHELSEA PLAYERS —

Fiona Richmond, 70s porn star (John Boyle)
Dee Dee Wilde, Pan's People dancer (Tommy Baldwin)
Dani Behr, TV presenter (Mark Bosnich)
Sophie Anderton, model (Mark Bosnich)
Alessia Rossi Andra, Italian model (Hernan Crespo)
Meg Matthews, ex-wife of Noel Gallagher (Frank Lampard)
Moran Atias, Miss Israel (Adrian Mutu)
Laura Andresean, porn star (Adrian Mutu)
Laura Franco, Argentinean TV star (Juan Sebastian Veron)
Magdalena Graaf, Swedish model (Magnus Hedman)
Noemie Lenoir, French supermodel (Claude Makelele)
Cassie Sumner, glamour model (Michael Essien)

— CHELSEA'S LEADING PREMIERSHIP SCORERS —

1992/93	Mick Harford, Graham Stuart	9 goals
1993/94	Mark Stein	13 goals
1994/95	John Spencer	11 goals
1995/96	John Spencer	13 goals
1996/97	Gianluca Vialli	9 goals
1997/98	Tore Andre Flo, Gianluca Vialli	11 goals
1998/99	Gianfranco Zola	13 goals
1999/2000	Tore Andre Flo, Gustavo Poyet	10 goals
2000/01	Jimmy Floyd Hasselbaink	23 goals
2001/02	Jimmy Floyd Hasselbaink	23 goals
2002/03	Gianfranco Zola	14 goals
2003/04	Jimmy Floyd Hasselbaink	12 goals
2004/05	Frank Lampard	13 goals
2005/06	Frank Lampard	16 goals
2006/07	Didier Drogba	20 goals

— SKIPPER RON'S RECORD —

As well as holding the record for the most appearances for the club, Ron 'Chopper' Harris has also captained Chelsea more times than any other player. Altogether, Harris wore the armband 324 times for the Blues – a total made up of 238 league games, 38 in the FA Cup, 22 in the League Cup, 25 in Europe and one Charity Shield fixture.

— GEORGE'S TRAVELS —

Former World Player of the Year George Weah is one of only two Chelsea players to have plied his trade on three continents: Africa, Europe and Asia. Weah's career began in his native Liberia on the coast of west Africa where he played for a number of clubs, including Young Survivors, Bongrange, Mighty Barole and Invincible Eleven. After a spell with Cameroon side Tonnerre Yaounde, George made the move to Europe, joining Monaco. Following big money transfers to PSG and AC Milan, he joined Chelsea on loan in January 2000. Despite a successful stint at the Bridge, where he picked up an FA Cup winner's medal, Weah moved on at the end of the season to Manchester City. He later played for Marseille, rejoined Monaco and then tried his luck in the Middle East with United Arab Emirates outfit Al-Jazirah.

The other onetime Blue to have played on three continents is occasional 1970s striker Derek Smethurst. Born in South Africa, Derek played for Durban City before joining Chelsea in December 1968. After making his debut for the Blues in 1970 and collecting a European Cup Winners Cup medal the following year, he moved on to Millwall in September 1971. Four years later Smethurst switched continents again, joining American outfit Tampa Bay Rowdies.

— FA VETO BLUES' EURO ADVENTURE —

In 1955 Chelsea, then reigning English league champions, were invited to take part in the inaugural contest of the European Cup. However, the Football Association were concerned that the new tournament would adversely affect the normal league season and advised Chelsea to withdraw. The Blues, who had already been drawn to play Swedish champions Djurgardens, followed the FA's advice and, as it turned out, had to wait until 1999 before finally taking part in European football's premier competition.

— TOMMY'S LATE ARRIVAL . . .
AND PREMATURE DEPARTURE —

On Christmas Day 1920 Chelsea's new signing from Manchester United, wing-half Tommy Meehan, turned up at Stamford Bridge fully expecting to make his debut for his new club against Liverpool. To his dismay, he found that the match, a 1–1 draw, had already been played that morning.

Tragically, Meehan died a few days before the start of the 1924/25 season. A memorial fund for his wife and children raised £1,500 thanks to contributions from 15 other League clubs. The fund was also boosted by a benefit match staged at Stamford Bridge on 20 October 1924 between Chelsea and a Football League XI.

— TV BLUES —

(Kerry) Dixon of Dock Green
The Morecambe and (Dennis) Wise Show
(John) Terry and June
Alas (Bobby) Smith and (Vinnie) Jones
(John) Dempsey and Makepeace
A Touch of (Lee) Frost
The Dukes of (Mickey) Hazard
George (Graham) and Mildred
(Terry) Howard's Way
Dan (Pet Rescue)

— SUBSTITUTE SKIPPER —

At Selhurst Park on 20 November 1971, Chelsea played the first 24 minutes of the match without their skipper, midfielder Steve Kember. Having taken part in the toss, Kember then took up his place on the substitutes' bench and only got involved in the action when he replaced the injured Tommy Baldwin. He then led the Blues to a 3-2 victory against the side he had left just two months earlier.

— HOME FROM HOME —

On two occasions Chelsea have played both the original FA Cup tie and the subsequent replay at Stamford Bridge. In 1915 the Blues were drawn at home to Southern League side Swindon in the first round. After a 1–1 draw, the replay a week later was also staged at the Bridge by mutual agreement, with Chelsea winning 5–2 after extra-time. Then, in 1994, Chelsea's third round away tie with Barnet was switched from the north Londoners' tiny Underhill stadium to Stamford Bridge on safety grounds. The match finished in a 0–0 draw before Chelsea won the replay, again at the Bridge, by a convincing 4–0 margin. Strangely, in both 1915 and 1994 Chelsea went on to finish as FA Cup runners-up.

— FINAL SHAME —

Only two Chelsea players have experienced the ignominy of being sent off in a major final. In the 1998 European Cup Winners Cup final in Stockholm Dan Petrescu was slightly unfortunate to be dismissed for a foul challenge on a Stuttgart player after 84 minutes. Nine years later, in the 2007 Carling Cup final between Chelsea and Arsenal at the Millennium stadium in Cardiff, John Obi Mikel was sent off after grappling with Gunners defender Kolo Toure. The Arsenal player was also shown the red card along with team-mate Emmanuel Adebayor, who was dismissed for his role in the mass brawl which followed the original incident.

— STRANGEST GOAL EVER? —

The most bizarre goal scored at Stamford Bridge, and quite possibly in the history of football, occurred during a game between Chelsea and Leicester City on 18 December 1954. In an attempt to clear the ball from their penalty area after John McNichol's shot had hit the bar, Leicester defenders Stan Milburn and Jack Froggatt only managed to send it spinning past their goalkeeper, John Anderson. The goal went down in the record books as 'Milburn and Froggatt shared own goal', the only known occasion when a goal has been credited in this way.

— CONSIDERABLY RICHER THAN YOU! —

Ten richest European clubs, according to the Deloitte Football Money List:

Club	Income*	Change on previous season
Real Madrid	£202.0m	+£15.8m
Barcelona	£179.1m	+£38.7m
Juventus	£173.7m	+£28.8m
Manchester Utd	£167.8m	+£1.4m

AC Milan	£165.0m	+£7.0m
Chelsea	**£152.8m**	**+£3.7m**
Inter Milan	£142.8m	+£23.1m
Bayern Munich	£141.5m	+£13.5m
Arsenal	£133.0m	+£17.3m
Liverpool	£121.7m	−£0.7m

*Figures based on the 2005/06 season

— HELLO, GOODBYE —

Ten Chelsea players who were swapped with ten others from rival clubs:

Year	Transferred player	Signed player	To/From
1946	Joe Payne	Harry Medhurst	West Ham
1959	Les Allen	Johnny Brooks	Tottenham
1959	Cliff Huxford	Charlie Livesey	Southampton
1961	Ron Tindall	Andy Malcolm	West Ham
1966	George Graham	Tommy Baldwin	Arsenal
1968	Joe Kirkup	David Webb	Southampton
1984	Tony McAndrew	Darren Wood	Middlesbrough
1992	Tommy Boyd	Tony Cascarino	Celtic
1993	Graeme Le Saux	Steve Livingstone	Blackburn
2003	Graeme Le Saux	Wayne Bridge	Southampton

— CHEERS, OLD CHUM! —

Four Chelsea players have scored for the club while not actually being on the pay-roll:

- In May 1978, three years after leaving the Bridge and five years before he returned, John Hollins scored for the Blues while playing for QPR. Chelsea won the game 3–1.
- In October 1984, two years after leaving Chelsea, Mickey Nutton scored for the Blues in their 3–1 defeat of Millwall in the League Cup.
- In February 1992, two years before he signed for Chelsea, Mal Donaghy netted for the Blues while playing for Manchester United in a 1–1 draw at Old Trafford.
- In August 1999, former Chelsea defender Frank Sinclair helpfully headed into his own net in the last minute to earn the Blues a point at Leicester.

— MEDAL-WINNING BOSSES —

The Chelsea managers who won the FA Cup in their playing days are:

David Calderhead (Notts County, 1894)
Ted Drake (Arsenal, 1936)
Danny Blanchflower (Tottenham, 1961 and 1962)
Geoff Hurst (West Ham, 1964)
Eddie McCreadie (Chelsea, 1970)
John Hollins (Chelsea, 1970)
David Webb (Chelsea, 1970)
Ian Porterfield (Sunderland, 1973)
Glenn Hoddle (Tottenham, 1981 and 1982)
Gianluca Vialli (Chelsea, 1997)

— CELEBS TURN OUT FOR BLUES IN LA —

During their 2006 American tour, Chelsea hosted a reception at the exclusive Sky Bar in Los Angeles. Among the A-list celebrities spotted chatting to Blues players at the star-studded event were:

Tony Blair, Prime Minister of Great Britain
Snoop Dogg, rapper
Serena and Venus Williams, tennis players
Jennifer Love Hewitt, actress
Brandon Flowers, lead singer with *The Killers*
Joshua Jackson, *Dawson's Creek* actor
Rick Fox, captain of the LA Lakers basketball team
Vidal Sassoon, hairdresser to the stars

— ZOLA IS GREATEST EVER —

In January 2003 Gianfranco Zola was voted Chelsea's best ever player in a poll of fans on the club's official website. The little Sardinian received a staggering 60 per cent of the votes, to put him a considerable distance ahead of the runner-up, 70s striker Peter Osgood. The top ten, which would presumably look very different if a similar poll was conducted today, was as follows:

1) Gianfranco Zola
2) Peter Osgood
3) Dennis Wise
4) Jimmy Greaves
5) Kerry Dixon
6) Ruud Gullit
7) Peter Bonetti
8) Charlie Cooke
9) Gianluca Vialli
10) Jimmy Floyd Hasselbaink

— FIRST 100 GAMES —

The ten most successful Chelsea managers over their first hundred games in charge are:

Manager	P	W	D	L	F	A	%
1. Jose Mourinho (2004-)	100	72	18	10	185	60	81.0
2. Gianluca Vialli (1998-2000)	100	54	26	20	155	80	67.0
3. Claudio Ranieri (2000-04)	100	50	27	23	183	107	63.5
4. Bobby Campbell (1988-91)	100	48	31	21	186	140	63.5
5. Dave Sexton (1967-74)	100	47	27	26	157	124	60.6
6. John Hollins (1985-88)	100	43	26	31	139	139	56.0
7. David Calderhead (1907-33)	100	45	17	38	159	147	53.5
8. Tommy Docherty (1961-67)	100	40	20	40	169	154	50.0
9. Glenn Hoddle (1993-96)	100	34	31	35	119	119	49.5
10=. Ted Drake (1952-61)	100	33	31	36	151	153	48.5
10=. John Neal (1981-85)	100	33	31	36	134	139	48.5

— OH NO, NOT YOU LOT AGAIN! —

Between 2001 and 2004 Chelsea were drawn to play Arsenal in the FA Cup in four consecutive seasons. The run began in the fifth round in 2001 when, despite a superb goal by Jimmy Floyd Hasselbaink, Arsenal won 3–1 at Highbury. The following year the Gunners beat Chelsea 2–0 at Cardiff in the final and it was déjà vu in 2003 when Arsenal beat the Blues 3–1 at Stamford Bridge in a sixth round replay. Amazingly, in 2004 it was Groundhog Day yet again as the Gunners came from a goal down at half-time to beat Chelsea 2–1 at Highbury in the fifth round. The run finally came to an end in 2005 when Newcastle knocked the Blues out of the FA Cup in a fifth round tie at St James' Park.

— EVERY SCHOOLBOY'S DREAM —

Chelsea players recall the goals that won the club major cup silverware:

"I saw Gordon Banks come off his line, and I threw myself at the ball, got a toe to it just as he came out, on the edge of the 18-yard box, and it went past him and kind of bobbled into the net."
Eddie McCreadie, on what proved to be the Blues' winning goal in the 1965 League Cup final against Leicester City

"The ball hit me on the cheek. I went up to head it in, and as I leaning forward, Leeds players got underneath me to try to put me off. I was determined to connect with the ball, and I knew that if I threw myself in the right spot, I'd score."
David Webb, describing his famous winner in the 1970 FA Cup final replay against Leeds

"Tommy Baldwin had the ball, he gave it to me and made a run forward. As he went he was screaming for me to knock it through, but all of a sudden a big gap opened up because he'd taken two of their defenders with him. I just bent it, the ball hit the post and went right in the corner."
Peter Osgood, recalling his winning goal in the 1971 European Cup Winners Cup final replay against Real Madrid

"I thought to myself maybe I will shoot. So I did. I was very lucky because when I hit the ball it went first up and the down behind the goalkeeper. I was so carried away I just couldn't calm down and it was unbelievable, the feeling, and also so great an emotion for me."
Roberto Di Matteo, on Chelsea's opening goal after just 43 seconds in the 1997 FA Cup final against Middlesbrough

"A lot of their players slowed down, they didn't think Wisey was going to get there. But I knew how quick he was and he put the ball on my head really."
Frank Sinclair, describing the build up to his opener in Chelsea's 2–0 victory over Middlesbrough in the 1998 Coca-Cola Cup final

"I thought, 'This is the moment, Franco, take it' and fortunately everything went right because I hit the ball perfectly and it went where I wanted it to go. It was absolutely magnificent."

Gianfranco Zola, on his spectacular winning goal in the 1998 European Cup Winners Cup final

"I was pleased that the goal went in. I've been lucky quite a few times now. It's a coincidence, it's luck, it's destiny – all of that."

Roberto Di Matteo gets all philosophical about his winner against Aston Villa in the 2000 FA Cup final

"It was a very special moment. The reaction of the fans was incredible and it felt great to score the goal that made them all so happy."

Mateja Kezman, recalling his winning goal against Liverpool in the 2005 Carling Cup final at the Millennium Stadium

"I just ran past the defender and anticipated the cross. When the cross is coming as fast as it came, it is easy for me to choose where to put the ball. When Robbie crossed, I knew I was going to score."

Didier Drogba, on the second of his two goals in Chelsea's 2007 Carling Cup victory over Arsenal

"I feel great. I'm just happy to score the first cup final goal in the new stadium."

Didier Drogba, on his winner against Manchester United in the 2007 FA Cup final at the new Wembley

— EUROPEAN RECORD —

Before the start of the 2007/08 season, Chelsea had taken part in 16 European campaigns. The first was in 1958/59 when the Blues reached the second round of the Fairs Cup before going out 4–2 on aggregate to Red Star Belgrade. The most successful were in 1970/71 and 1997/98 when Chelsea won the European Cup Winners Cup with victories over Real Madrid and Stuttgart respectively.

For many years the Blues had a proud unbeaten home record in Europe, remaining undefeated at Stamford Bridge for 33 matches (27 wins, 6 draws) between 1958 and 2000. That record was finally ended by Lazio who won 2–1 at the Bridge in a Champions League second group stage match on 22 March 2000. Since then, only Besiktas (Champions League group stage, 2003) and Barcelona (Champions League last 16, 2006) have beaten Chelsea on their home turf.

Overall, Chelsea's European record reads:

	P	W	D	L	F	A
Home	62	44	15	3	133	35
Away	64	23	16	25	81	76
Neutral	4	3	1	0	5	2
Total	130	70	32	28	219	113

— MUSICAL FANS —

Celebrity Chelsea fans in the music business include:

Bryan Adams
Damon Albarn (Blur)
Lloyd Cole
Paul Cook (Sex Pistols)
Dave Gahan (Depeche Mode)
Geri Halliwell (Spice Girls)
Paul Hardcastle
Morten Harket (A-Ha)
Nik Kershaw
Gary Numan
Suggs (Madness)

— CHARITY BEGINS AT THE BRIDGE —

In 1908 the first ever Charity Shield match was played at Stamford Bridge, between league champions Manchester United and Southern League champions QPR. After a 1–1 draw, United won the replay 4–0. The matches raised £1,275 for charitable causes.

The following three Charity Shields were also held at the Bridge, which has been the venue for 10 of these games in total. The most recent was in 1970 when FA Cup winners Chelsea lost 2–1 at home to league champions Everton.

— THE FIRST FOREIGNER —

Danish international Nils Middelboe was the first player from outside Britain or Ireland to play for Chelsea. A Danish international defender, he came to London on business before World War I and, looking for a club to play for, signed for Chelsea as an amateur in 1913.

'The Great Dane', as he was known, played for the Blues for nine years and became an inspirational captain, although his business interests often meant he was unavailable for selection. Outside wartime friendlies, Middlelboe only made 46 appearances for the club but he made a big impression on his team-mates, who presented him with a silver cigarette box when he returned to Denmark in 1922.

Throughout his time at the Bridge Middelboe refused to accept a penny from the club in return for his services. Asked once by the Chelsea secretary what his expenses were, he replied: "Expenses? I ought to pay the club for providing a fine afternoon's sport."

— A MARATHON AND A SPRINT —

In the 2006/07 season Chelsea played a club record 64 matches: 38 in the Premiership, 12 in the Champions League, seven in the FA Cup, six in the Carling Cup and one in the Community Shield. Midfielder Frank Lampard set a club appearance record by playing in 62 of the games (58 starts plus four as sub).

By contrast, in five pre-World War 1 seasons Chelsea played just 40 matches: 38 in the league and two in the FA Cup.

— FLYING HIGH —

On 19 April 1957 Chelsea became the first English club to travel by air to a Football League match. The new experience seemed to suit the Blues who won 2–1 at Newcastle with goals from Derek Saunders and Les Stubbs. The following day there was no sign of jet lag either, as Chelsea thrashed Everton 5–1 at the Bridge.

— A RECORD-BREAKING SEASON 2 —

The last time Chelsea were promoted to the top flight, back in season 1988/89, they went up with a then record number of points for the old Second Division, 99. The Blues' impressive tally stood for 10 years until Sunderland amassed a total of 105 points in 1998/99.

Second Division Top Six 1988/89

	P	W	D	L	F	A	Pts
Chelsea	46	29	12	5	96	50	99
Manchester City	46	23	13	10	77	53	82
Crystal Palace	46	23	12	11	71	49	81
Watford	46	22	12	12	74	48	78
Blackburn Rovers	46	22	11	13	74	59	77
Swindon Town	46	20	16	10	68	53	76

— SPORTY BLUES —

So popular are Chelsea among practitioners of other sports the Blues could almost enter their own Olympic team of celebrity fans. Among the most famous sports people to follow the club are:

Alec Stewart, Graham Thorpe, Shane Warne (Cricket)
Pat Cash, Boris Becker (Tennis)
Jimmy White, Tony Drago (Snooker)
Lawrence Dallaglio, Brian Moore, Sir Clive Woodward (Rugby Union)
Dick Francis, Clare Balding (Horse racing)
Johnny Herbert (Motor racing)
Joe Calzaghe (Boxing)
Eric Bristow (Darts)
Daley Thompson (Athletics)
Sir Steven Redgrave (Rowing)

— HAT-TRICK HEROES —

No fewer than 61 Chelsea players have scored hat-tricks for the Blues, the most recent member of this prestigious club being midfielder Frank Lampard who scored three times against Macclesfield at the Bridge on 6 January 2007. The most prolific scorer of hat-tricks is legendary hit-man Jimmy Greaves who struck an incredible 13 in just 169 appearances for the Blues – an average of one every 13 games!

Player	Number of hat-tricks	Appearances
Jimmy Greaves	13	169
George Hilsdon	9	164
Bobby Tambling	8	370
Kerry Dixon	8	420
Peter Osgood	5	380

— MILESTONE MATCHES* —

100th league game: Chelsea 0 Nottingham Forest 4 (18 January 1908)
200th league game: Chelsea 2 Birmingham City 2 (12 November 1910)
300th league game: Liverpool 1 Chelsea 2 (24 March 1913)
500th league game: Manchester City 0 Chelsea 0 (25 March 1922)
1,000th league game: Chelsea 0 Sheffield Wednesday 1 (17 March 1934)
2,000th league game: West Bromwich Albion 0 Chelsea 2 (5 December 1964)
3,000th league game: Watford 1 Chelsea 2 (6 November 1988)

* Includes the three games played at the start of the abandoned 1939/40 season which are sometimes discounted from official records

— ROVERS' SENSE OF HUMOUR FAILURE —

On 5 May 1996 Blackburn Rovers made an official complaint to Chelsea after the Blues' matchday programme published humorous pen portraits of their players. Among the tongue-in-cheek comments to annoy the Rovers players and management were:

Tim Flowers: He used to answer the phone saying, "Safest hands in football . . ." Just his little joke.

Bobby Mimms: The man Tottenham fans called 'The Cat', because he gave them all kittens.

Chris Coleman: After the 2–0 defeat in Switzerland, Bobby Gould's Welsh spies were seen checking the birth registers again – desperately trying to prove that the Blackburn defender was eligible to play for Ireland.

Alan Shearer: Not since John Wayne Bobbitt have a man's private parts been the subject of so much concern to the male population of England – that groin operation's recovery time is vital to the nation's chances in Euro' 96.

— GIVE US A GAME, DAD! —

Remember when Fergie kept picking Darren Ferguson for the Manchester United team even though, to most observers at least, his son wasn't up to the required level?

Well, long-serving Chelsea boss David Calderhead also faced accusations of nepotism when his son, David jnr, was on the Stamford Bridge books between 1911 and 1914. Never a regular, David jnr made just 43 appearances at centre-half for the Blues during his three years at Chelsea.

— LONDON MONARCHS —

In December 1996 the London Monarchs American Football team played their first match at Stamford Bridge, having previously performed at Wembley Stadium and White Hart Lane. The following season, in 1997, the Monarchs played all of their home games in the National Football League of Europe at the Bridge, a venue familiar to their field kicker: former Chelsea striker Clive Allen. It wasn't a great season for the Monarchs, though, as the league table reveals:

		P	W	L
1)	Rhein Fire	10	7	3
2)	Barcelona Dragons	10	5	5
3)	Scottish Claymores	10	5	5
4)	Amsterdam Admirals	10	5	5
5)	Frankfurt Galaxy	10	4	6
6)	London Monarchs	10	4	6

The following season the team left the Bridge and, after changing its name to England Monarchs, played its home matches at Crystal Palace, Bristol and Birmingham. In 1998 the team was withdrawn from the NFL (Europe) and replaced by Berlin Thunder.

— GOING DOWN, GOING DOWN, GOING DOWN! —

On two occasions Chelsea have relegated teams from the Premiership by beating them at Stamford Bridge on the last day of the season. In 1994 the Blues came from behind to defeat Sheffield United 3–2, thanks to a last-minute Mark Stein goal. The result meant the Blades were relegated instead of Ipswich.

Four years later, in 1998, Chelsea beat Bolton 2–0 at the Bridge to send the Trotters down. The home crowd, though, would have preferred to have seen Everton relegated and chanted "let 'em score!" as Bolton mounted a series of desperate attacks in the closing minutes. Sadly for the Trotters, the Blues' defence ignored the chants.

— TOTTENHAM HOODOO —

Chelsea were unbeaten in 32 league meetings against London rivals Tottenham between 1990 and 2007, their longest such run against any club. The sequence began with a 3-2 victory for the Blues at Stamford Bridge on 1 December 1990 and finally came to an end with a 2-1 defeat at White Hart Lane on 5 November 2007.

Of the 32 games between the clubs during that period Chelsea won 21 and drew 11, scoring 63 goals and conceding just 23 in the process. The Blues' leading scorer during their phenomenal run was Jimmy Floyd Hasselbaink with 10 goals, including a hat-trick in a 4-0 home win over Spurs in March 2002.

— GOALS GALORE 2 —

Although Chelsea have only scored ten or more goals just once in a competitive match, the Blues have hit double figures on a number of occasions in friendlies and unofficial fixtures:

Year	Result	Fixture category
1964	St James (Jamaica) 0 Chelsea 15	Friendly
2001	Cascia (Italy) 0 Chelsea 14	Friendly
1965	Tasmania (Australia) 0 Chelsea 12	Friendly
1964	St Mary's (Jamaica) 1 Chelsea 12	Friendly
2000	Reggioteam (Holland) 0 Chelsea 11	Friendly
1916	Chelsea 11 Luton Town 1	Wartime league
1943	QPR 2 Chelsea 11	Wartime league
1972	Barbados Combined XI 0 Chelsea 10	Friendly
1994	Kingstonian 0 Chelsea 10	Friendly

— CHAIRMAN'S UNSUNG HERO AWARD —

In 1994 Ken Bates established an annual chairman's award for the club's 'unsung hero'. The winners of the award are:

1994 Kevin Hitchcock
1995 David Lee
1996 Gwyn Williams
1997 Terry Byrne
1998 Gustavo Poyet
1999 Gianluca Vialli
2000 Antonio Pintus
2001 Claudio Ranieri
2002 John Terry and Jody Morris

— THE YOUNG WONS —

Chelsea have won the FA Youth Cup on two occasions, in 1960 and 1961. Among those who played in at least one of these finals were Terry Venables, Bert Murray, Bobby Tambling, Peter Bonetti and Ron Harris, all of whom went on to enjoy long careers with the Blues:

Year	Results
1960	Chelsea 1 Preston North End 1
	Preston North End 1 Chelsea 4 (2–5 on agg)
1961	Chelsea 4 Everton 1
	Everton 2 Chelsea 1 (3–5 on agg)

— COLIN'S RED ARM BAND —

During the 1985/86 season Chelsea skipper Colin Pates broke with convention by wearing a red arm band, rather than a black one. He explained why in the home programme against Fulham in October 1985: "A few people have asked me about the red arm band I've been wearing this season so here's the explanation: some referees have been asking team captains to wear identification this season and as I don't like to wear morbid black, Norman Medhurst (*team trainer*) made a red arm band for me out of an old sock." However, the old sock got the boot when Pates was replaced as skipper by Joe McLaughlin at the start of the 1987/88 season.

— BIG FISH V SMALL FRY —

Chelsea have played numerous friendlies against non-league opposition over the years. Despite being apparent mismatches, results have not always gone the way of the Blues – as these scores indicate:

1906	Chelsea 0 London Caledonians 1
1924	Chelsea 0 Corinthians 2
1974	Hastings United 2 Chelsea 1
1979	Weymouth 2 Chelsea 1
1981	Woking 2 Chelsea 2
1989	Keynsham Town 0 Chelsea 0
1993	Chesham United 4 Chelsea 1

— YOU ARE THE WEAKEST LINK...GOODBYE! —

Two former Chelsea players, Peter Bonetti and Graeme Le Saux, have appeared on the popular TV quiz show 'The Weakest Link'. In 2001 Bonetti was one of nine former footballers who braved the acid tongue of presenter Anne Robinson in a special charity edition of the show. 'The Cat' survived to the last five before being voted off. Martin Chivers, the onetime Tottenham and England striker, won the contest.

In 2005 Graeme Le Saux did even better in a sports stars edition of 'The Weakest Link'. He beat off competition from the likes of hurdler Colin Jackson, rower James Cracknell and *Grandstand* host Steve Rider to reach the final, before losing out to BBC horse racing presenter and Chelsea fan Clare Balding.

— TEAM OF TEAMS —

During the 2003/04 and 2004/05 seasons the Chelsea matchday programme ran a regular feature called 'My Chelsea XI'. For each home game a distinguished former player or coach would be asked to nominate their favourite Blues eleven in whatever formation they preferred. Among the 54 interviewees were great names such as Peter Osgood, Peter Bonetti, Roy Bentley, Dennis Wise and Kerry Dixon. The team of players collecting the most votes lined up as follows:

Peter Bonetti (24 votes)

Ron Harris (19)   **John Terry** (38)   **Marcel Desailly** (28)

Dennis Wise (20)

Steve Clarke (18)   **Charlie Cooke** (20)
Frank Lampard (20)   **Eddie McCreadie** (22)

Peter Osgood (25)   **Gianfranco Zola** (45)

Subs: **Alan Hudson** (17), **Jimmy Greaves** (15), **Ruud Gullit** (14), **Kerry Dixon** (14), **Graeme Le Saux** (14), **Ray Wilkins** (13)

— FIRST NAME ON THE TEAMSHEET...ME! —

The only players to pick themselves in the same poll (see *Team of Teams*, above) were 1955 championship winner Stan Willemse, 70s legends Alan Hudson and Marvin Hinton, and 80s stars Nigel Spackman and Clive Walker. The quintet gave the following reasons for their slightly egotistical choices:

Marvin Hinton: "I know it's a little bit arrogant to put myself in, and it's difficult to leave out Ron Harris and Demps (John Dempsey), but the system I like has a strong centre-back alongside someone to pick up the pieces and that's something I was ideal at."

Alan Hudson: "Every team I ever pick, I pick myself. I can't be left out."

Nigel Spackman: "Player-coach. I just want to play with the other players. I'm a goalscoring midfielder really – in disguise!"

Clive Walker: "65 goals from the left-wing. No further comment. I don't want to talk about me but there's not a chance I'm going to miss out on playing with this team. Plus I've got to keep reminding people about my playing days."

Stan Willemse: "I had to pick myself as I so enjoyed playing in this (1955) team."

— BLUE DOUBLE WINNERS —

Chelsea have never won the Double of league championship and FA Cup, but a number of Blues players have done so with other teams, either before or after moving to Stamford Bridge:

Player	Club	Year
Bobby Smith	Tottenham	1961
Les Allen	Tottenham	1961
George Graham	Arsenal	1971
Mark Hughes	Manchester United	1994
Paul Parker	Manchester United	1994
Emmanuel Petit	Arsenal	1998
Ashley Cole	Arsenal	2002

— STALWARTS REWARDED —

Chelsea have given many long-serving players well-deserved testimonials. Here is a selection of results from those matches:

Player	Year	Result
Ken Shellito	1968	Chelsea 6 QPR 3
Peter Bonetti	1971	Chelsea 1 Standard Liege 2
Peter Houseman	1973	Chelsea 4 Fulham 1
Eddie McCreadie	1974	Chelsea 1 Manchester United 2
John Hollins	1974	Chelsea 1 Arsenal 1
Peter Osgood	1975	Chelsea 4 Chelsea Past XI 3
Marvin Hinton	1976	Chelsea 2 Crystal Palace 2
Ian Hutchinson	1978	Chelsea 2 QPR 2
Charlie Cooke	1978	Chelsea 2 Crystal Palace 0
Peter Bonetti	1979	Chelsea 5 Manchester United 3
John Dempsey	1980	Chelsea 5 International XI 3
Ron Harris	1980	Chelsea 0 Chelsea Past XI 1
Mickey Droy	1983	Chelsea 2 Arsenal 1
John Bumstead	1987	Chelsea 1 Real Sociedad 0
Colin Pates	1988	Chelsea 0 Tottenham 0
Eddie Niedzwiecki	1989	Chelsea 5 Chelsea 1984/85 4
Kerry Dixon	1995	Chelsea 5 Tottenham 1
Paul Elliott	1995	Chelsea 1 Porto 1
Steve Clarke	1996	Chelsea 2 PSV 3
Kevin Hitchcock	1998	Chelsea 3 Nottingham Forest 3
Dennis Wise	1999	Chelsea 0 Bologna 0
Gianfranco Zola*	2004	Chelsea 3 Real Zaragoza 0

* Tribute match

— 1-0 TO CHELSEA...AGAIN —

In the seasons since the Premiership was formed in 1992/93, Chelsea's most common league results have been:

1992/93: Drew 1-1 (8 times)
1993/94: Drew 1-1 (9 times)
1994/95: Drew 1-1 (7 times)
1995/96: Drew 1-1 (7 times)
1996/97: Drew 1-1 (6 times)
1997/98: Won 2-0 and Lost 1-0 (6 times each)
1998/99: Won 2-1 (7 times)
1999/2000: Won 1-0 (9 times)
2000/01: Won 3-0, Lost 2-0 and Drew 1-1 (4 times each)

2001/02: Drew 0-0 (6 times)
2002/03: Drew 1-1 (6 times)
2003/04: Won 1-0 (10 times)
2004/05: Won 1-0 (11 times)
2005/06: Won 2-0 (10 times)
2006/07: Won 1-0 (9 times)

— THEY SAID IT —

"I'm not a good darts player myself, I've tried it and I could barely hit the board."

Darts fan Arjen Robben, September 2005

"I had a couple of glasses of champagne. I had a little dance with my wife. She is a better dancer than me. But the best dancer in the management team is Peter Kenyon. Honestly!"

Jose Mourinho, describing how he celebrated Chelsea's 2006 Premier League title triumph, April 2006

"It wasn't over a girl. It wasn't down to any reason I could think of. It was a case of falling asleep in the wrong place."

Joe Cole, after being beaten up at a party, January 2006

"I just love football and like to watch it whenever I can, even if my girlfriend would prefer to watch *EastEnders*."

John Terry, March 2006

"Man United came in quite early for me. But really I saw the possibilities at Chelsea being much greater – a stronger team – and also London has its attractions as a family man."

Michael Ballack, explaining his decision to move from Bayern to the Bridge, May 2006

— PREMIERSHIP CHAMPIONS 2006 —

Chelsea won back-to-back league titles for the first time in season 2005/06, confirming their triumph with an emphatic 3-0 victory over Manchester United at Stamford Bridge. The Blues' home form was sensational throughout the campaign, with only Charlton managing to leave SW6 undefeated. At the end of the season the Premiership table looked like this:

	P	W	D	L	F	A	W	D	L	F	A	Pts
Chelsea	38	18	1	0	47	9	11	3	5	25	13	91
Man Utd	38	13	5	1	37	8	12	3	4	35	26	83
Liverpool	38	15	3	1	32	8	10	4	5	25	17	82
Arsenal	38	14	3	2	48	13	6	4	9	20	18	67
Tottenham	38	12	5	2	31	16	6	6	7	22	22	65
Blackburn	38	13	3	3	31	17	6	3	10	20	25	63
Newcastle	38	11	5	3	28	15	6	2	11	19	27	58
Bolton	38	11	5	3	29	13	4	6	9	20	28	56
West Ham	38	9	3	7	30	25	7	4	8	22	30	55
Wigan	38	7	3	9	24	26	8	3	8	21	26	51
Everton	38	8	4	7	22	22	6	4	9	12	27	50
Fulham	38	13	2	4	31	21	1	4	14	17	37	48
Charlton	38	8	4	7	22	21	5	4	10	19	34	47
Middlesbrough	38	7	5	7	28	30	5	4	10	20	28	45
Man City	38	9	2	8	26	20	4	2	13	17	28	43
Aston Villa	38	6	6	7	20	20	4	6	9	22	35	42
Portsmouth	38	5	7	7	17	24	5	1	13	20	38	38
Birmingham	38	6	5	8	19	20	2	5	12	9	30	34
West Brom	38	6	2	11	21	24	1	7	11	10	34	30
Sunderland	38	1	4	14	12	37	2	2	15	14	32	15

— THE LONG AND THE SHORT OF IT —

Lanky Dutch goalkeeper Ed de Goey is the tallest player in Chelsea history. Standing at 6ft 6in, Ed is just one inch taller than the Blues' current No 1, Petr Cech.

The shortest player to appear for the Blues is Jackie Crawford. The 1920s inside forward was a mere 5ft 3in tall.

— THE BLUES' GREATEST MOMENTS . . . EVER! —

In 2005, the club's centenary year, Chelsea TV invited fans to vote for their three favourite moments in the Blues' history. When all the votes were counted up this was the Top 20:

1. Frank Lampard's goals at Bolton secure the Premiership title, 2005
2. Wayne Bridge's late winner knocks Arsenal out of the Champions League, 2004
3. Roberto di Matteo's 43-second opener sets up FA Cup glory, 1997
4. Roman Abramovich buys Chelsea, 2003
5. David Webb wins first FA Cup for the Blues, 1970
6. Gianfranco Zola nets with a backheel volley against Norwich, 2002
7. Blues fight back from 2-0 down to beat Liverpool in the FA Cup, 1997
8. Zola scores the winner in European Cup Winners Cup final, 1998
9. Peter Osgood's diving header in the FA Cup Final replay, 1970
10. Chelsea FC are formed, 1905
11. Chelsea beat Barcelona 4-2 in one of the all-time great games, 2005
12. The Blues lift FA Cup at the old Wembley for the last time, 2000
13. The Blues beat Liverpool to gain Champions League qualification, 2003
14. Ruud Gullit signs for Chelsea to begin an era of foreign stars at the Bridge, 1995
15. Clive Walker's winner saves the Blues from the drop to Division Three, 1983
16. The Blues stuff Lazio 4-0 in Rome, 2003
17. Treble winners Manchester United are humbled 5-0 at the Bridge, 1999
18. The Bridge is saved from the grasping hands of property developers, 1992
19. A first league win at Highbury for 15 years, 2005
20. Zola hits a cup semi special against Wimbledon, 1997

— MISCELLANEOUS SEASONAL RECORDS —

Highest points total: 99, 1988/89
Most league wins: 29, 1988/89, 2004/05 and 2005/06
Most home wins: 18, 1906/07 and 2005/06
Most away wins: 15, 2004/05
Fewest defeats: 1, 2004/05
Fewest home defeats: 0, 1910/11, 1976/77, 2004/05, 2005/06 and 2006/07
Fewest away defeats: 1, 2004/05

Lowest points total: 20, 1978/79
Fewest league wins: 5, 1978/79
Fewest home wins: 3, 1978/79
Fewest away wins: 0, 1914/15
Most defeats: 27, 1978/79
Most home defeats: 13, 1978/79
Most away defeats: 16, 1961/62

Most goals scored: 98, 1960/61
Most goals scored at home: 61, 1960/61
Most goals scored away: 46, 1988/89
Fewest goals conceded: 15, 2004/05
Fewest goals conceded at home: 6, 2004/05
Fewest goals conceded away: 9, 2004/05

Fewest goals scored: 31, 1923/24
Fewest goals scored at home: 17, 1921/22
Fewest goals scored away: 8, 1923/24
Most goals conceded: 100, 1960/61
Most goals conceded at home: 50, 1959/60
Most goals conceded away: 65, 1961/62

Most draws: 18, 1922/23
Most home draws: 13, 1922/23
Most away draws: 9, on eight occasions
Fewest draws: 3, 1997/98
Fewest home draws: 0, 1906/07
Fewest away draws: 1, 1962/63 and 1997/98

— HANDBAGS AT TEN PACES —

Football's a passionate game so it's not surprising that, over the years, Chelsea players and staff have been involved in a number of violent incidents on the pitch. Here are some of the most memorable clashes:

- **Ted Drake and Stan Cullis (Wolves)**: The two bosses came to blows after Chelsea's dramatic 4-3 win at Molineux in December 1954. "Ted approached Cullis ready to shake his hand," recalled Blues skipper Roy Bentley. "Stan, stubborn as ever, refused and muttered something under his breath. Ted replied with his fists and landed a punch that knocked Stan over."

- **Eddie McCreadie and Francesco Carpenetti (Roma)**: In a tempestuous Fairs Cup clash at the Bridge in October 1965 left-back McCreadie was sent off in the first half for throwing a punch at an opponent. "I went on an overlap, got my cross in, and this guy came across and kicked me in the shins," remembered Eddie. "Then he put his hand right round my throat. And I was, well, have some of that, you know. And I decked him." Despite being reduced to ten men, Chelsea still won the game 4–1.

- **Mickey Thomas and Andy Blair (Sheffield Wednesday)**: In only his second game for the Blues following his transfer from Stoke in January 1984, Thomas reacted to taunts from the Wednesday midfielder about the end of his turbulent marriage to a former Miss Wales runner up. "He was dishing out loads of stick during the game so in the end I cracked and knocked him clean out with one punch," recalled Thomas. "The ref and linesmen didn't see it but the Chelsea fans were cheering and singing, 'There's only one Mickey Thomas'."

- **Nigel Spackman and Martin Keown (Arsenal)**: The normally mild-mannered Spackers was sent off after whacking the Arsenal defender towards the end of the Blues 1-0 win at the Bridge in September 1995. "Martin Keown tried to elbow me and missed, and I just lost it and punched him," he said later. "That was very unlike me. But I'd had a bad week as my little lad Frazer had just been diagnosed with cerebral palsy. I got a three-match ban for violent conduct. It was embarrassing, but I got the best standing ovation I've ever had as a left the pitch."

- **Chelsea and Wimbledon**: After a bad-tempered London derby at the Bridge in February 2000 at least 16 players became involved in a mass punch up in the tunnel as they headed towards their changing rooms. During the fracas, Wimbledon boss Egil Olsen was knocked to the floor and the fighting was only halted when police intervened. Chelsea attempted to downplay the incident, although assistant manager Gwyn Williams admitted, "Someone fell down the stairs and there was a scuffle." Both clubs were charged with misconduct by the FA and Chelsea were later fined £50,000 for their part in the affair. Blues skipper Dennis Wise, whose on-pitch clash with Wimbledon's Kenny Cunningham sparked the tunnel war, was also fined £7,500.

- **Chelsea and Arsenal**: The two sides were charged with misconduct after an injury-time brawl during the Blues' Carling Cup victory. The confrontation was sparked when Chelsea midfielder John Obi Mikel grabbed Kolo Toure's shirt and the Arsenal player reacted angrily. As the incident threatened to spiral out of control, Blues boss Jose Mourinho and Gunners manager Arsene Wenger rushed onto the pitch to act as peacemakers. After order was restored, referee Howard Webb sent off Mikel, Toure and another Arsenal player, Emanuel Adebayor, while Blues stand-in skipper Frank Lampard and Arsenal midfielder Cesc Fabregas were booked.

— CUP HOLDERS KO'D —

Chelsea have knocked out the reigning cup holders in the following competitions:

FA Cup

Year	Round	Result
1931	4th	Chelsea 2 Arsenal 1
1965	4th	West Ham 0 Chelsea 1
1966	3rd	Liverpool 1 Chelsea 2

League Cup

Year	Round	Result
1965	Final	Chelsea 3 Leicester City 2 (aggregate)
1971/72	Semi-final	Chelsea 5 Tottenham 4 (aggregate)

European Cup Winners Cup

Year	Round	Result
1971	Semi-final	Chelsea 2 Manchester City 0 (aggregate)

— PATHS TO GLORY —

Chelsea have won ten major cup competitions. Here are the full details of those successes . . .

FA CUP 1970

3rd round	Birmingham City	(H)	W	3-0
4th round	Burnley	(H)	D	2-2
Replay	Burnley	(A)	W	3-1 (aet)
5th round	Crystal Palace	(A)	W	4-1
6th round	QPR	(A)	W	4-2
Semi-final	Watford (White Hart Lane)		W	5-1
Final	Leeds (Wembley)		D	2-2 (aet)
Replay	Leeds (Old Trafford)		W	2-1 (aet)

FA CUP 1997

3rd round	West Bromwich Albion	(H)	W	3-0
4th round	Liverpool	(H)	W	4-2
5th round	Leicester City	(A)	D	2-2
Replay	Leicester City	(H)	W	1-0 (aet)
6th round	Portsmouth	(A)	W	4-1
Semi-final	Wimbledon (Highbury)		W	3-0
Final	Middlesbrough (Wembley)		W	2-0

FA CUP 2000

3rd round	Hull City	(A)	W	6-1
4th round	Nottingham Forest	(H)	W	2-0
5th round	Leicester City	(H)	W	2-1
6th round	Gillingham	(H)	W	5-0
Semi-final	Newcastle United (Wembley)		W	2-1
Final	Aston Villa (Wembley)		W	1-0

FA CUP 2007

3rd round	Macclesfield	(H)	W	6-1
4th round	Nottingham Forest	(H)	W	3-0
5th round	Norwich City	(H)	W	4-0
6th round	Tottenham	(H)	D	3-3
Replay	Tottenham	(A)	W	2-1
Semi-final	Blackburn (Old Trafford)		W	2-1 (aet)
Final	Manchester United (Wembley)		W	1-0 (aet)

LEAGUE CUP 1965

2nd round	Birmingham City	(A)	W	3-0
3rd round	Notts County	(H)	W	4-0
4th round	Swansea Town	(H)	W	3-2
5th round	Workington Town	(A)	D	2-2
Replay	Workington Town	(H)	W	2-0
Semi-final (1)	Aston Villa	(A)	W	3-2
Semi-final (2)	Aston Villa	(H)	D	1-1
Final (1)	Leicester City	(H)	W	3-2
Final (2)	Leicester City	(A)	D	0-0

LEAGUE (COCA-COLA) CUP 1998

3rd round	Blackburn	(H)	D	1-1 (aet, won 4-1 on pens)
4th round	Southampton	(H)	W	2-1 (aet)
5th round	Ipswich	(A)	D	2-2 (aet, won 4-1 on pens)
Semi-final (1)	Arsenal	(A)	L	1-2
Semi-final (2)	Arsenal	(H)	W	3-1
Final	Middlesbrough (Wembley)		W	2-0 (aet)

LEAGUE (CARLING) CUP 2005

3rd round	West Ham United	(H)	W	1-0
4th round	Newcastle United	(A)	W	2-0 (aet)
5th round	Fulham	(A)	W	2-1
Semi-final (1)	Manchester United	(H)	D	0-0
Semi-final (2)	Manchester United	(A)	W	2-1
Final	Liverpool (Millennium stadium)		W	3-2 (aet)

LEAGUE (CARLING) CUP 2007

3rd round	Blackburn	(A)	W	2-0
4th round	Aston Villa	(H)	W	4-0
5th round	Newcastle United	(A)	W	1-0
Semi-final (1)	Wycombe	(A)	D	1-1
Semi-final (2)	Wycombe	(H)	W	4-0
Final	Arsenal (Millennium stadium)		W	2-1

EUROPEAN CUP WINNERS CUP 1971

1st round (1)	Aris Salonika	(A)	D	1-1
1st round (2)	Aris Salonika	(H)	W	5-1
2nd round (1)	CSKA Sofia	(A)	W	1-0
2nd round (2)	CSKA Sofia	(H)	W	1-0
Quarter-final (1)	Bruges	(A)	L	0-2
Quarter- final	(2) Bruges	(H)	W	4-0 (aet)
Semi-final (1)	Manchester City	(H)	W	1-0
Semi-final (2)	Manchester City	(A)	W	1-0
Final	Real Madrid (Athens)		D	1-1 (aet)
Replay	Real Madrid (Athens)		W	2-1

EUROPEAN CUP WINNERS CUP 1998

1st round (1)	Slovan Bratislava	(H)	W	2-0
1st round (2)	Slovan Bratislava	(A)	W	2-0
2nd round (1)	Tromso	(A)	L	2-3
2nd round (2)	Tromso	(H)	W	7-1
Quarter-final (1)	Betis	(A)	W	2-1
Quarter-final (2)	Betis	(H)	W	3-1
Semi-final (1)	Vicenza	(A)	L	0-1
Semi-final (2)	Vicenza	(H)	W	3-1
Final	Stuttgart (Stockholm)		W	1-0

— FIRST FOREIGN OPPONENTS —

Chelsea's first non-English opponents were Sparta Rotterdam, who played a friendly at Stamford Bridge on 17 April 1906. The Dutch side, who at the time were a powerful force in their domestic league, won the match 2-0.

— HEY, HEY, WE'RE THE MONKEYS —

In the late 1990s Bristol Zoo named four black howler monkeys after Chelsea players. The baby monkey monikers – Zola (born 1997), Desailly (1998), Babayaro (1999) and Vialli (2000) – were chosen by primate overseer John Buchan, a committed fan of the Blues.

— GIFT-WRAPPED GOALS —

Prior to the start of the 2007/08 season, the last ten opposition players to score own goals for Chelsea were:

Year	Comp	Player	Result
2007	Prem	Abel Xavier	Chelsea 3 Middlesbrough 0
2007	Prem	Chris Kirkland	Chelsea 4 Wigan 0
2006	Prem	Liam Rosenior	Chelsea 2 Fulham 2
2006	Prem	Ivar Ingimarsson	Reading 0 Chelsea 1
2006	CL	Thiago Motta	Chelsea 1 Barcelona 2
2005	Prem	Zurab Khizanishvili	Chelsea 4 Blackburn 2
2005	Carl	Steven Gerrard	Chelsea 3 Liverpool 2*
2005	CL	Juliano Belletti	Barcelona 2 Chelsea 1
2005	FA	Andy Crosby	Chelsea 3 Scunthorpe 1
2004	Prem	James Beattie	Chelsea 2 Southampton 1

* after extra-time

— SOMETHING SHINY FOR THE MANTELPIECE —

Major individual awards presented to Chelsea players and managers:

African Player of the Year: George Weah, 1989 (with Monaco), 1994 (with Paris St Germain, shared), 1995 (with AC Milan); Didier Drogba, 2006
European Footballer of the Year: Ruud Gullit, 1987 (with AC Milan), George Weah, 1995 (with AC Milan); Andriy Shevchenko, 2004 (with AC Milan)
FA Premier League Manager of the Year: Jose Mourinho, 2005 and 2006
FIFA World Footballer of the Year: George Weah, 1995 (with AC Milan)
(Football Writers' Association) Footballer of the Year: Gianfranco Zola, 1997; Frank Lampard, 2005
(PFA) Footballer of the Year: Clive Allen, 1987 (with Tottenham); Mark Hughes, 1989 and 1991 (with Manchester United); John Terry, 2005
World Footballer of the Year (*World Soccer*): Ruud Gullit, 1987 and 1989 (with AC Milan), Gianluca Vialli, 1995 (with Juventus)
World Manager of the Year (*World Soccer*): Terry Venables, 1985 (with Barcelona); Jose Mourinho, 2004 (with Porto and Chelsea) and 2005

— BLUES IN RED —

A team of Chelsea players who also turned out at Old Trafford:

1. Alex Stepney (1966)
2. Paul Parker (1997)
3. Harold Halse (1914-21)
4. Juan Sebastian Veron (2003-)
5. Mal Donaghy (1992-94)
6. Ray Wilkins (1973-79)
7. Jim McCalliog (1964-65)
1. Tommy Baldwin (1966-74)
9. George Graham (1964-66)
10. Mark Hughes (1995-98)
11. Mickey Thomas (1984-85)

Manager: Tommy Docherty (1961-67)

— CHELSEA'S ALL-TIME LEAGUE RECORD AGAINST 2007/08 PREMIERSHIP CLUBS —

			Home					Away			
	P	W	D	L	F	A	W	D	L	F	A
Arsenal	140	22	25	23	83	91	17	19	34	88	113
Everton	136	35	21	12	126	64	14	21	20	89	146
Man Utd	130	19	17	29	93	112	17	23	25	68	101
Liverpool	128	36	13	15	116	65	8	13	43	66	137
Newcastle	126	36	17	10	123	67	13	16	34	63	98
Man City	124	30	20	12	102	67	19	16	27	71	90
Aston Villa	120	31	11	18	87	69	13	18	29	81	113
Tottenham	118	28	12	19	83	74	22	5	22	88	97
Middlesbrough*	102	33	13	5	97	37	11	16	24	53	83
Sunderland	100	32	11	7	105	50	13	9	28	58	99
Bolton	96	24	12	12	85	57	13	14	21	66	89
Blackburn*	94	24	11	12	87	56	13	14	20	51	67
Derby County	92	20	15	11	73	53	12	10	24	56	84
West Ham	78	19	7	13	71	59	10	7	22	50	75
Birmingham	76	20	12	6	69	40	14	11	13	61	63
Portsmouth	68	16	12	6	71	48	12	9	13	50	55
Fulham	56	16	10	2	46	22	17	6	5	51	31
Reading	10	2	3	0	5	3	2	1	2	8	9
Wigan	4	2	0	0	5	0	2	0	0	4	2

* Includes 1987/88 play-off matches

— WE LOVE YOU CHELSEA —

"Chelsea has always been my first love. I'd have liked to have spent the whole of my career at Stamford Bridge, but it was not to be. I always have a special place in my football heart for Chelsea."

1960s captain Terry Venables

"Becoming a Chelsea director was one of the most marvellous things that has happened in my life."

Lord Attenborough

"The blue and the blue, with white socks – it was smart. It wasn't just Chelsea, it was smart."

1970s defender David Webb

"Chelsea FC will never lose its identity. Chelsea will be Chelsea for always – and at Stamford Bridge."

Chelsea chairman Brian Mears, April 1977

"I walk in here every day and you look out there and you get a tingling down your back. It's a tremendous set-up. Tremendous supporters."

John Neal, on his appointment as manager in 1981

"Managing Chelsea Football Club is without doubt the proudest moment in my football career so far."

Glenn Hoddle, in his last programme notes before becoming England manager, May 1996

"To wear the colours of Chelsea must be an honour,"

Ruud Gullit in August 1996, shortly after his appointment as player/manager.

"You Chelsea supporters have been unbelievable to me so far. I can't ask you for anything more now that I am player/manager."

Gianluca Vialli, after taking over as manager, February 1998

"Hello, Chelsea supporters. You may not have heard of me before I came to you last month, but I had heard of you. I knew that Chelsea are a good team in Europe and that the fans are great."

Claudio Ranieri, in his first programme notes, October 2000

"It feels good because it's a change, it's a big challenge, and I'm playing with players like Zola who I've been a massive fan of for years. To mix with players like that and train with them is brilliant."
Frank Lampard, shortly after joining Chelsea, July 2001

"You don't get many one-club players nowadays, but I definitely want to stay at Chelsea for the rest of my career."
John Terry, November 2001

"I played for Napoli and it was blue. I play for Chelsea and it's blue. Italy is blue. Blue belongs to me, my life."
Gianfranco Zola, January 2002

"As soon as I arrived here I instantly had a great feeling, it filled me with confidence, and it was clear to me I had to decide to come to Chelsea."
Arjen Robben, December 2004

"I'm very happy here. I see myself as a Chelsea player for a long time."
Petr Cech, November 2005

"At some clubs you just play for them and then once you're gone that's it, but the new regime at Chelsea has remembered that there were 99 years of history before they arrived."
Pat Nevin, January 2006

"If I'm still here, I hope I can be just like the old boys of '55 who came out and celebrated with us last season. They came with a lot of dignity, enjoyed their football, and I hope that will be me. I think I'll still be living in the area and watching Chelsea."
Frank Lampard looks forward 50 years, December 2005

"Sometimes I laugh when I hear some of the things the fans sing about me during games. But it's lovely."
Claude Makelele, January 2007

"I went along and said, 'If you want me to do it, I'll do it. But I have to be a Chelsea supporter.'"
Phil Daniels on his role as Blues fan Kevin Wicks in *EastEnders*

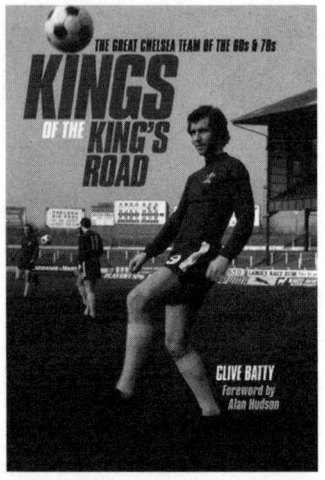
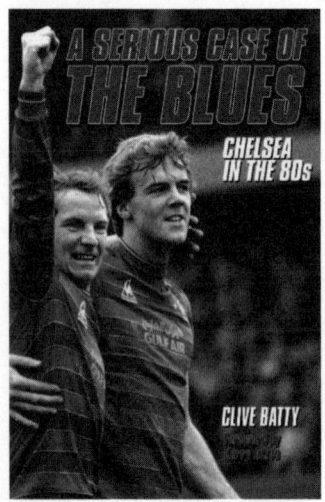

— CHELSEA'S LEAGUE RECORD 1905-2007 —

	Div	P	W	D	L	F	A	W	D	L	F	A	Pts	Pos
1905/06	2	38	13	4	2	58	16	9	5	5	32	21	53	3rd
1906/07	2	38	18	0	1	55	10	8	5	6	25	24	57	2nd
														(Promoted)
1907/08	1	38	8	3	8	30	35	6	5	8	23	27	36	13th
1908/09	1	38	8	7	4	33	22	6	2	11	23	39	37	11th
1909/10	1	38	10	4	5	32	24	1	3	15	15	46	29	19th
														(Relegated)
1910/11	2	38	17	2	0	48	7	3	7	9	23	28	49	3rd
1911/12	2	38	15	2	2	36	13	9	4	6	26	21	54	2nd
														(Promoted)
1912/13	1	38	7	2	10	29	40	4	4	11	22	33	28	18th
1913/14	1	38	12	3	4	28	18	4	4	11	18	37	39	8th
1914/15	1	38	8	6	5	32	25	0	7	12	19	40	29	19th
1915/19						FIRST WORLD WAR								
1919/20	1	42	15	3	3	33	10	7	2	12	23	41	49	3rd
1920/21	1	42	9	7	5	35	24	4	6	11	13	34	39	18th
1921/22	1	42	9	6	6	17	16	8	6	7	23	27	46	9th
1922/23	1	42	5	13	3	29	20	4	5	12	16	33	36	19th
1923/24	1	42	7	9	5	23	21	2	5	14	8	32	32	21st
														(Relegated)
1924/25	2	42	11	8	2	31	12	5	7	9	20	35	47	5th
1925/26	2	42	10	7	4	42	22	9	7	5	34	27	52	3rd
1926/27	2	42	13	7	1	40	17	7	5	9	22	35	52	4th
1927/28	2	42	15	2	4	46	15	8	6	7	29	30	54	3rd
1928/29	2	42	10	6	5	40	30	7	4	10	24	35	44	9th
1929/30	2	42	17	3	1	49	14	5	8	8	25	32	55	2nd
														(Promoted)
1930/31	1	42	13	4	4	42	19	2	6	13	22	48	40	12th
1931/32	1	42	12	4	5	43	27	4	4	13	26	46	40	12th
1932/33	1	42	9	4	8	38	29	5	3	13	25	44	35	18th
1933/34	1	42	12	3	6	44	24	2	5	14	23	45	36	19th
1934/35	1	42	11	5	5	49	32	5	4	12	24	50	41	12th
1935/36	1	42	11	7	3	39	27	4	6	11	26	45	43	8th
1936/37	1	42	11	6	4	36	21	3	7	11	16	34	41	13th
1937/38	1	42	11	6	4	40	22	3	7	11	25	43	41	10th
1938/39	1	42	10	5	6	43	29	2	4	15	21	51	33	20th
1939/46						SECOND WORLD WAR								

Season	Div	P	W	D	L	F	A	W	D	L	F	A	Pts	Pos
1946/47	1	42	9	3	9	33	39	7	4	10	36	45	39	15th
1947/48	1	42	11	6	4	38	27	3	3	15	15	44	37	18th
1948/49	1	42	10	6	5	43	27	2	8	11	26	41	38	13th
1949/50	1	42	7	7	7	31	30	5	9	7	27	35	40	13th
1950/51	1	42	9	4	8	31	25	3	4	14	22	40	32	20th
1951/52	1	42	10	3	8	31	29	4	5	12	21	43	36	19th
1952/53	1	42	10	4	7	35	24	2	7	12	21	42	35	19th
1953/54	1	42	12	3	6	45	26	4	9	8	29	42	44	8th
1954/55	1	42	11	5	5	43	29	9	7	5	38	28	52	1st (Champions)
1955/56	1	42	10	4	7	32	26	4	7	10	32	51	39	16th
1956/57	1	42	7	8	6	43	36	6	5	10	30	37	39	13th
1957/58	1	42	10	5	6	47	34	5	7	9	36	45	42	11th
1958/59	1	42	13	2	6	52	37	5	2	14	25	61	40	14th
1959/60	1	42	7	5	9	44	50	7	4	10	32	41	37	18th
1960/61	1	42	10	5	6	61	48	5	2	14	37	52	37	12th
1961/62	1	42	7	7	7	34	29	2	3	16	29	65	28	22nd (Relegated)
1962/63	2	42	15	3	3	54	16	9	1	11	27	26	52	2nd (Promoted)
1963/64	1	42	12	3	6	36	24	8	7	6	36	32	50	5th
1964/65	1	42	15	2	4	48	19	9	6	6	41	35	56	3rd
1965/66	1	42	11	4	6	30	21	11	3	7	35	32	51	5th
1966/67	1	42	7	9	5	33	29	8	5	8	34	33	44	9th
1967/68	1	42	11	7	3	34	25	7	5	9	28	43	48	6th
1968/69	1	42	11	7	3	40	24	9	3	9	33	29	50	5th
1969/70	1	42	13	7	1	36	18	8	6	7	34	32	55	3rd
1970/71	1	42	12	6	3	34	21	6	9	6	18	21	51	6th
1971/72	1	42	12	7	2	41	20	6	5	10	17	29	48	7th
1972/73	1	42	9	6	6	30	22	4	8	9	19	29	40	12th
1973/74	1	42	9	4	8	36	29	3	9	9	20	31	37	17th
1974/75	1	42	4	9	8	22	31	5	6	10	20	41	33	21st (Relegated)
1975/76	2	42	7	9	5	25	20	5	7	9	28	34	40	11th
1976/77	2	42	15	6	0	51	22	6	7	8	22	31	55	2nd (Promoted)
1977/78	1	42	7	11	3	28	20	4	3	14	18	49	36	16th
1978/79	1	42	3	5	13	23	42	2	5	14	21	50	20	22nd (Relegated)
1979/80	2	42	14	3	4	34	16	9	4	8	32	36	53	4th

Season	Div	P	W	D	L	F	A	W	D	L	F	A	Pts	Pos
1980/81	2	42	8	6	7	27	15	6	6	9	19	26	40	12th
1981/82*	2	42	10	5	6	37	30	5	7	9	23	30	57	12th
1982/83	2	42	8	8	5	31	22	3	6	12	20	39	47	18th
1983/84	2	42	15	4	2	55	17	10	9	2	35	23	88	1st (Promoted)
1984/85	1	42	13	3	5	38	20	5	9	7	25	28	66	6th
1985/86	1	42	12	4	5	32	27	8	7	6	25	29	71	6th
1986/87	1	42	8	6	7	30	30	5	7	9	23	34	52	14th
1987/88	1	40	7	11	2	24	17	2	4	14	26	51	42	18th (Relegated)
1988/89	2	46	15	6	2	50	25	14	6	3	46	25	99	1st (Promoted)
1989/90	1	38	8	7	4	31	24	8	5	6	27	26	60	5th
1990/91	1	38	10	6	3	33	25	3	4	12	25	44	49	11th
1991/92	1	42	7	8	6	31	30	6	6	9	19	30	53	14th
1992/93	Pr	42	9	7	5	29	22	5	7	9	22	32	56	11th
1993/94	Pr	42	11	5	5	31	20	2	7	12	18	33	51	14th
1994/95	Pr	42	7	7	7	25	22	6	8	7	25	33	54	11th
1995/96	Pr	38	7	7	5	30	22	5	7	7	16	22	50	11th
1996/97	Pr	38	9	8	2	33	22	7	3	9	25	33	59	6th
1997/98	Pr	38	13	2	4	37	14	7	1	11	34	29	63	4th
1998/99	Pr	38	12	6	1	29	13	8	9	2	28	17	75	3rd
1999/00	Pr	38	12	5	2	35	12	6	6	7	18	22	65	5th
2000/01	Pr	38	13	3	3	44	20	4	7	8	24	25	61	6th
2001/02	Pr	38	11	4	4	43	21	6	9	4	23	17	64	6th
2002/03	Pr	38	12	5	2	41	15	7	5	7	27	23	67	4th
2003/04	Pr	38	12	4	3	34	13	12	3	4	33	17	79	2nd
2004/05	Pr	38	14	5	0	35	6	15	3	1	37	9	95	1st (Champions)
2005/06	Pr	38	18	1	0	47	9	11	3	5	25	13	91	1st (Champions)
2006/07	Pr	38	12	7	0	37	11	12	4	3	27	13	83	2nd

* Three points for a win introduced 1981/82